Conquering Second Grade

Reading
Mathematics
Science
Social Studies
Writing

Kristy Stark, M.A.Ed.

Publishing Credits

Corinne Burton, M.A.Ed., *President*; Conni Medina, M.A.Ed., *Managing Editor;* Emily R. Smith, M.A.Ed., *Content Director*; Lynette Ordoñez, *Editor*; Angela Johnson, M.F.A., M.S.Ed., *Editor*; Evan Ferrell, *Graphic Designer*; Lubabah Memon, *Assistant Editor*

Image Credits

pp. 7, 22, 26, 34, 37, 64, 68, 82, 90, 113, 116 Illustrations by Timothy J. Bradley; all other images from iStock and/or Shutterstock.

Standards

Shell Education
A division of Teacher Created Materials
5301 Oceanus Drive
Huntington Beach, CA 92649-1030

www.tcmpub.com/shell-education
ISBN 978-1-4258-1621-6

Table of Contents

Dear Family,

Welcome to *Conquering Second Grade*. Second grade will be an exciting and challenging year for your child. This book is designed to supplement the concepts your child is learning in second grade and to strengthen the connection between home and school. The activities in this book are based on today's standards and provide practice in reading, word study, language, writing, mathematics, social studies, and science. It also features fun, yet challenging, critical-thinking activities and games. In addition to the activity sheets in this book, the end of each section also provides engaging extension activities.

Your child should complete one unit per month, including the extension activities. This will allow your child to think about grade-level concepts over a longer period of time. This also ensures that the book can be completed in one school year.

Keep these tips in mind as you work with your child this year:

- Set aside specific times each week to work on the activities.
- Have your child complete one or two activities each time rather than an entire unit at one time.
- Keep all practice sessions with your child positive and constructive. If the mood becomes tense or if you and your child get frustrated, set the book aside and find another time to practice.
- Help your child with instructions, if necessary. If your child is having difficulty understanding what to do, work through some of the problems together.
- Encourage your child to do his or her best work, and compliment the effort that goes into learning.

Enjoy the time learning with your child during second grade. Summer will be here before you know it!

Sincerely,

The Shell Education Staff

Suggested Family Activities

Extend your child's learning by taking fun family field trips. A wide variety of experiences helps develop a child's vocabulary. Field trips also provide greater context and meaning to his or her learning in school.

A Trip to a Zoo

Bring a blank paper on a clipboard with you. Fold the paper into four even squares, and label them Desert, Ocean, Rainforest, and Forest. Have your child guess which biome each animal belongs in and write the animal's name in the right square. Then, have your child read the information placard and determine if he or she is correct.

A Trip to a Museum

Your first stop should be the gift shop. Have your child pick five postcards of artifacts or paintings in the museum. Then, as you visit the museum, your child should be on the lookout for the five items he or she chose. It's an individual scavenger hunt! If your child finds all five items, you can celebrate the accomplishment! Plus, your child gets to keep the postcards as mementos of the day.

A Trip to a Library

Ask your child about a new skill he or she is interested in learning. Your child can then use the digital catalog to search for books about this skill that match his or her reading level. Have your child choose two books about the topic, check them out, and enjoy learning a new skill!

A Trip to a National Park

The National Park Service has a great program called Junior Rangers. If you go to a local park, check in with the rangers at the visitors center to see what tasks your child can complete to earn a Junior Ranger patch and/or certificate. Your child can also go to the WebRangers site (www.nps.gov/webrangers/) and check out a vacation spot, play games, and earn virtual rewards!

A Trip to a Farmers' Market

Farmers' markets are great places to learn how different fruits and vegetables are grown. For each fruit or vegetable stand, have your child identify whether it is grown in the ground, on a bush, or on a tree. Encourage your child to ask the seller or farmer about the steps it takes to grow the plant. Have your child choose a fruit or vegetable he or she learned about to buy and enjoy with dinner that night!

Suggested Family Activities *(cont.)*

By discussing the activities in this book, you can enhance your child's learning. But it doesn't have to stop there. The suggestions below provide even more ideas on how to support your child's education.

General Skills

- Make sure your child gets plenty of exercise. Children need about 60 minutes of physical activity each day. You may want to have your child sign up for a sport. Or you can do fun things as a family, such as swimming, riding bicycles, or hiking.

- Help your child become organized and responsible. Have places for your child to keep important things. Take time to set up a schedule together. Use a timer to keep track of time spent on different activities.

Reading Skills

- Set a reading time for the entire family at least once every other day. Help your child choose a book at a comfortable reading level. Take turns reading aloud one page at a time. Be sure to help him or her sound out and define unfamiliar words.

- After reading, talk to your child about what he or she has read. Encourage your child to share details from the books.

Writing Skills

- Set up a writing spot for your child. Have all of his or her writing materials in one special place. Having a designated area to write will help your child see writing as an important activity.

- Encourage your child to write emails, texts, or letters to friends and family members who live near and far.

Mathematics Skills

- Encourage your child to practice telling time. Give your child an allotted amount of time to do an activity he or she enjoys. Ask your child to use a clock to figure out how long he or she has to do this activity. For example: *What will the clock look like when your 15 minutes of video games are up?*

- Include your child in grocery shopping. Use the prices in the store to ask your child questions. For example: *Apples are 50 cents each. If you have two dollars, how many apples can you buy?*

Directions: Read the text, and answer the questions.

Class Rules

My teacher has rules for our class. The rules keep us safe and make sure we can all learn. One rule is to not run inside. This rule was made so no one will get hurt. I think my teacher really cares about us. The rules keep us in order, so I follow them every day.

1. Who has to follow the teacher's rules?
   - (A) the student
   - (B) the teacher
   - (C) the principal
   - (D) the whole class

2. Which new title best fits the text?
   - (A) "A Caring Student"
   - (B) "Running Is Not Fun"
   - (C) "Following the Rules"
   - (D) "Breaking the Rules"

3. What is the root word in *teacher*?
   - (A) teach
   - (B) each
   - (C) eacher
   - (D) cher

4. What does the phrase *in order* mean in the text?
   - (A) quiet
   - (B) in a line
   - (C) behaved
   - (D) in a circle

Directions: Read the text, and answer the questions.

Safety First

"Why do I have to wear a bike helmet?" Lola asked.

"Your helmet helps keep you safe," said her mom. "If you fall, the helmet will protect your head. It is a law, too. You could get a ticket if you are caught riding without a helmet."

"Oh!" Lola said. "I don't want a ticket. I will be safe and wear my helmet."

1. What are Lola and her mom talking about?
   - (A) head injuries
   - (B) bike helmets
   - (C) tickets
   - (D) laws

2. What is the main idea?
   - (A) It is easy to fall off your bike.
   - (B) Helmets protect your head.
   - (C) Tickets are given if you break the law.
   - (D) Wearing a helmet is safe, and it is the law.

3. How would the word *helmet* be divided into two syllables?
   - (A) he-lmet
   - (B) h-elmet
   - (C) helm-et
   - (D) hel-met

4. Which of these words means the same as *protect*?
   - (A) lose
   - (B) expose
   - (C) guard
   - (D) injure

UNIT 1

High-Frequency Words

Directions: Write each word. Then, write each word backward.

1. country
2. every
3. add
4. plant
5. below
6. food
7. between
8. last
9. near
10. own

UNIT 1

Language

Directions: Circle the word that is spelled correctly in each set.

1	flight	flite	flyte
2	taugh	tawt	taught
3	squair	square	sqware
4	brought	brot	brawt
5	fixture	fixter	fixtcher
6	clewn	clown	cloun
7	needet	neded	needed
8	each	eche	eatch
9	watsh	wach	watch
10	fence	fens	fense

Directions: Think of three of your friends. Write the name of each friend. Then, list one thing you do with each friend.

My friend is: ______________________________

What my friend and I do: ____________________

____

____

My friend is: ______________________________

What my friend and I do: ____________________

____

____

My friend is: ______________________________

What my friend and I do: ____________________

____

____

UNIT 1

Writing

Directions: Describe a time when you played with a friend. Draw a picture to go with your narrative. Use your notes from page 11 to help you.

Remember!

A strong narrative includes:

- an introductory sentence
- sentences that describe the events
- names of specific people and places

Directions: Solve each problem.

1. $10 - 7 =$ ________

2. $\begin{array}{r} 4 \\ +\ 5 \\ \hline \square \end{array}$

3. $\begin{array}{r} \square \\ -\ 0 \\ \hline 10 \end{array}$

4. Find the difference between 8 and 6.

____

5. $10 - 1 = 9 - \square$

6. $6 + 2 =$ ________

7. $\begin{array}{r} 6 \\ -\ 1 \\ \hline \square \end{array}$

8. $\begin{array}{r} 8 \\ +\ 1 \\ \hline \square \end{array}$

9. Find the sum of 4 and 2.

____

10. $8 - 4 = \square + 2$

Directions: Solve each problem.

1. Write the numeral. Each bundle has 10 sticks. ________

2. Write the numeral.

2	hundreds	3	tens	5	ones

____

3. Write the numeral thirty-nine. ________

4. Write the numeral. Each bundle has 10 sticks. ________

5. Write the numeral sixty-seven. ________

6. Write the numeral.

4	tens	2	ones

____

7. Write the numeral ninety-three. ________

8. Write the number 71 in words. ________

Directions: Look at the example. Draw only the outline of each base-ten block. Then, solve the problems.

Example: Draw hundreds, tens, and ones to show 243.

Number	Hundreds	Tens	Ones
243	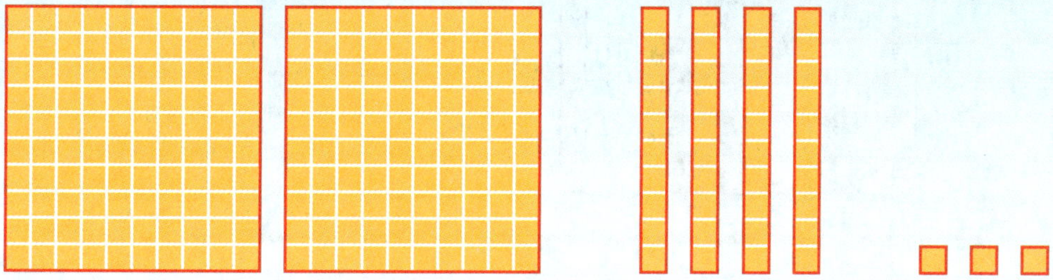		

Problems: Draw hundreds, tens, and ones to show 165 and 253.

	Hundreds	Tens	Ones
165			
253			

Directions: Show two ways to solve the problem. Draw only the outline of each base-ten block. Then, answer the question.

1. Connor is using base-ten blocks to show 236.

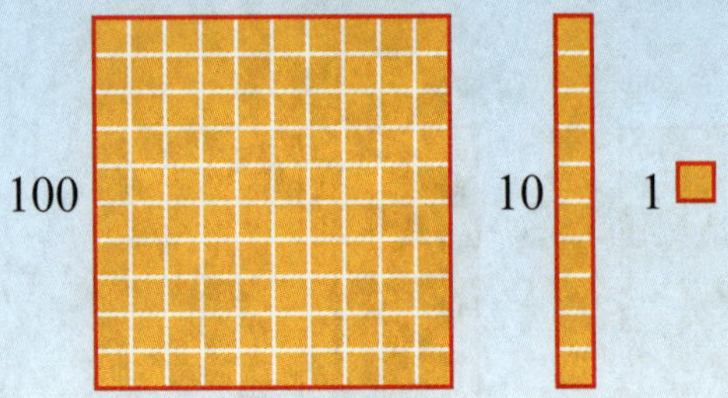

Strategy 1: Show the number using tens and ones.

Strategy 2: Show the number using hundreds, tens, and ones.

2. How are the two strategies different?

____

____

____

Directions: Look at the types of transportation listed in the box. Decide whether each type of transportation is used to move people, goods, or both. Write each type of transportation in the Venn diagram.

Types of Transportation

- car
- bus
- cargo ship
- train
- bicycle
- airplane
- scooter
- delivery truck

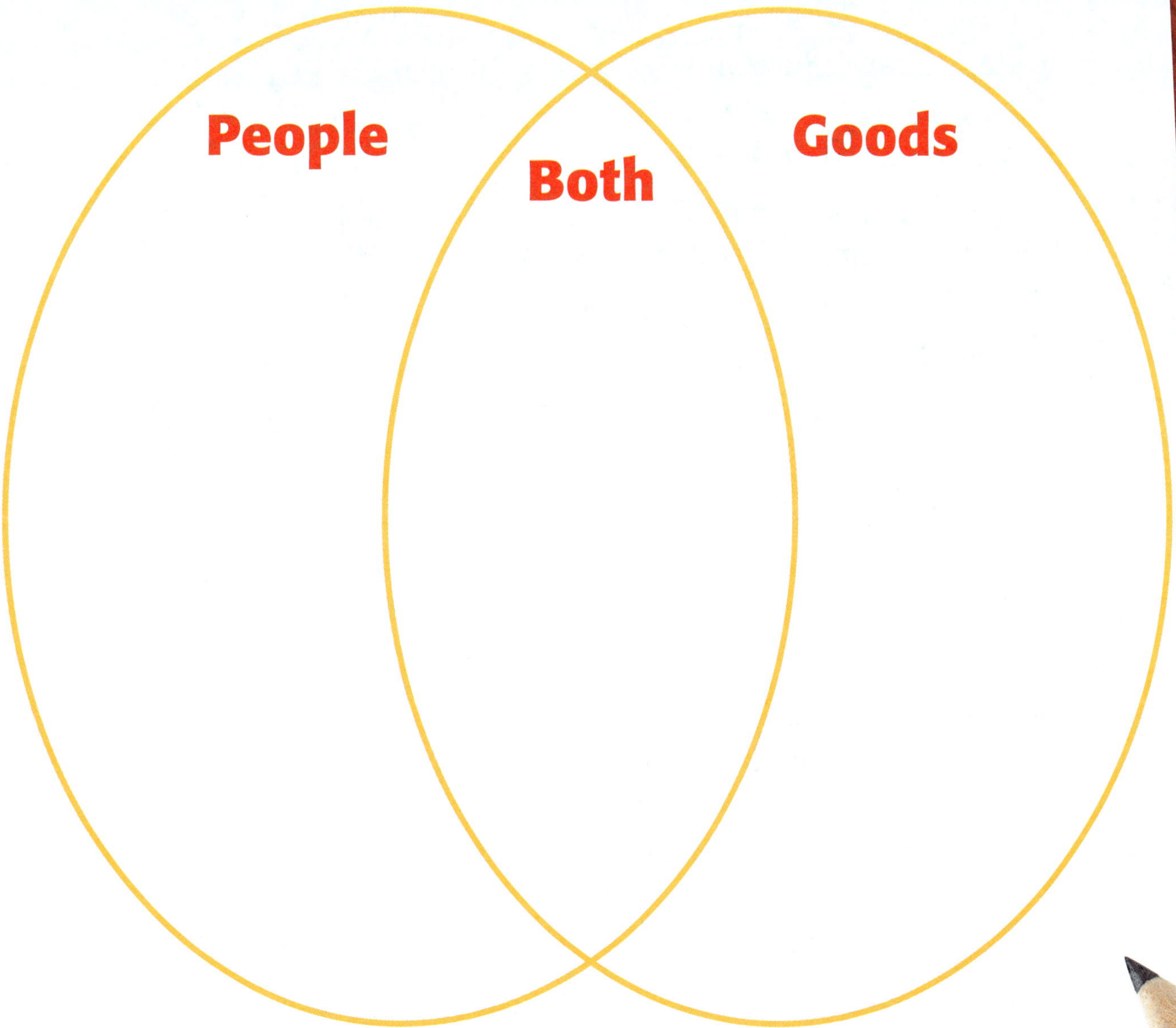

Directions: Follow the steps in this experiment to discover what happens when ice melts.

What You Need

- clear plastic cup
- water
- 1 ice cube
- marker

What to Do

1. Put an ice cube in your cup. Fill your cup halfway with water. Draw a line on your cup to show how full it is.
2. Does the ice float or sink? ____________________
3. Draw the water and ice in the cup. Show how much of the ice is below the water.

4. Draw your cup after the ice melts. Show the water level and the line you drew on your cup.

Directions: Solve each riddle.

1. I am an even number between 324 and 328. What number am I?

   ____

2. I am a shape. I have 4 right angles. I have 4 sides that are equal in length. What shape am I?

   ____

3. I am an odd number between 2 and 7. If you add 6 to me, you get a double-digit number. What number am I?

   ____

4. I am an even number. If you add me to 43, you get 67. What number am I?

   ____

5. I am a shape with an even number of sides. I have six vertices. What shape am I?

   ____

6. I am an odd number. I am the sum of 11 and 12. What number am I?

   ____

Directions: Roll three number cubes. For each roll, write a three-digit number that reflects the numbers on the cubes. Then, draw a picture that shows how many hundreds, tens, and ones are in each number. Use the example below to help you.

Number	Blocks
421	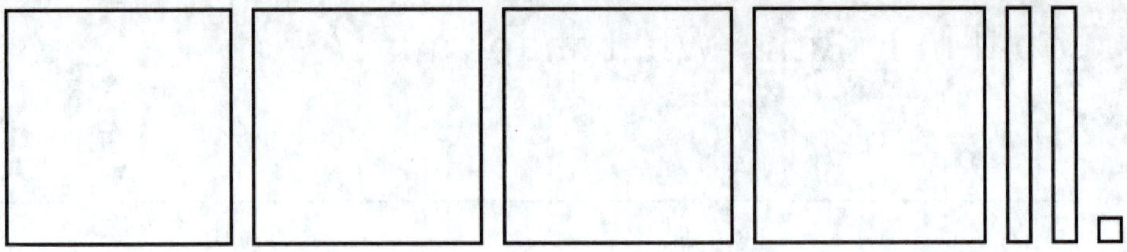

High-Frequency Words Activity

Write a funny sentence using the words from page 9.

Mathematics Activity

Choose a three-digit number. Represent it in at least three different ways.

Social Studies Activity

Look for different types of transportation as you walk or ride to somewhere. Make a list of all the types you see.

Science Activity

Fill a plastic cup halfway with water. Mark a line to show the water level. Place it in the freezer for one hour, and observe what happens. Is the ice above or below the line?

Critical-Thinking Activity

Write ten of your own riddles. Give your paper to a family member. Ask him or her to solve your riddles.

Listening-and-Speaking Activity

Write a speech about your favorite type of transportation. Record a podcast of your speech to share with your family.

Directions: Read the text, and answer the questions.

Felix's Nature Box

Felix has a special collection. He adds many items. They go into a nature box. He finds things on walks. Items catch his eye. Some days, he sees a rock. Other times, he finds a stick. He sees pretty flowers. Felix is proud of his collection.

1. Where does Felix find items for his nature box?
   - (A) in a box
   - (B) on his walks
   - (C) at home
   - (D) at school

2. What is the main topic?
   - (A) eyes
   - (B) a collection
   - (C) walking
   - (D) flowers

3. What is the root word in *collection*?
   - (A) lection
   - (B) coll
   - (C) lect
   - (D) collect

4. What does the phrase *catch his eye* mean in the text?
   - (A) get his attention
   - (B) poke him in the eye
   - (C) look at him
   - (D) sparkle in the sun

Directions: Read the text, and answer the questions.

Sorting!

My teacher said that mathematics is all around us. I was not sure what she meant. She told us to think about how we sort toys at home. My teacher told us to put them into different categories. My mom helped me. We sorted all my toys into groups. I made a special chart that showed the groups. My teacher really liked my work.

1. Who is the narrator of the text?
   - (A) a student
   - (B) a teacher
   - (C) a principal
   - (D) a mom

2. Which new title best describes the main idea?
   - (A) "A Teacher's Words"
   - (B) "Fun with Toys"
   - (C) "Mathematics in the Real World"
   - (D) "Categories at Home"

3. What is the root word in *showed*?
   - (A) show
   - (B) how
   - (C) howed
   - (D) owe

4. What did the teacher mean when she said mathematics is *all around us*?
   - (A) Mathematics time goes on all day.
   - (B) Mathematics work is never done.
   - (C) Mathematics is about what is in the air.
   - (D) Mathematics is found in the real world.

Directions: Read each sentence, and highlight the words from the Word Bank. Then, fill in the bubble next to the sentence that makes sense.

Word Bank

• school	• keep	• never	• people	• morning
• father	• tree	• house	• brother	• climb

1. Ⓐ I like to keep my room clean.
   Ⓑ The house will keep on the corner.

2. Ⓐ A school of fish swam in the sea.
   Ⓑ A school is where fish help people.

3. Ⓐ The fish climbed the tree to get away from the cat.
   Ⓑ The tree in my yard fell during the storm.

4. Ⓐ I have to ask my father if I can go to the movie.
   Ⓑ Dana can run father than her little brother, Tony.

5. Ⓐ There are never 70 minutes in an hour.
   Ⓑ The sun never rises every morning.

Directions: Fill in the bubble next to the correct answer.

1. What is the correct contraction?
   - Ⓐ weren't
   - Ⓑ wev'e
   - Ⓒ its'

2. What is another way to write *a bone belonging to a dog*?
   - Ⓐ a dogs bone
   - Ⓑ a dog's bone
   - Ⓒ a dogs' bone

3. What is another way to write *the party of a friend*?
   - Ⓐ a friend's party
   - Ⓑ party a friends party
   - Ⓒ a friend,s party

4. What is another way to write *the book belonging to my teacher*?
   - Ⓐ my teachers book
   - Ⓑ my teachers' book
   - Ⓒ my teacher's book

5. Which sentence is correct?
   - Ⓐ Jeff's work is very special to him.
   - Ⓑ Jeffs' work is very special to him.
   - Ⓒ Jeff's work' is very special to him.

6. Which contraction means "cannot"?
   - Ⓐ cann't
   - Ⓑ ca'nt
   - Ⓒ can't

7. What is the correct contraction?
   - Ⓐ Ih've
   - Ⓑ Iv'e
   - Ⓒ I've

8. Which contraction means "she has"?
   - Ⓐ she'd
   - Ⓑ she'll
   - Ⓒ she's

Directions: Look at the picture of a scarecrow. In what ways is it scary? In what ways is it not scary? Use words and pictures to describe your answers to the questions.

Scary Detail	Scary Detail
Not Scary Detail	**Not Scary Detail**

Directions: Do you think scarecrows are scary? Write a paragraph stating your opinion. Include supporting details and a picture to support your opinion. Use your notes on page 26 to help you.

Remember!

An opinion paragraph includes:

- an introductory sentence stating your opinion
- support for your opinion
- a concluding sentence

Directions: Solve each problem.

1. What is the place value of 7 in 71? ________________

2. Write the numeral for six hundred forty-three.

____

3. Write the numeral.

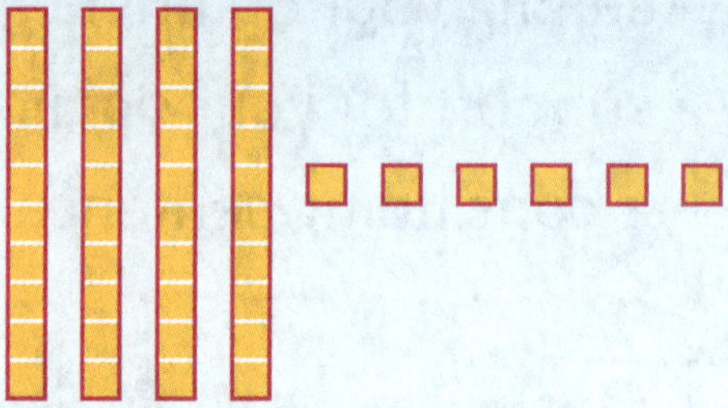

____

4. Circle the smaller number.

148 184

5. Write the numeral.

4	hundreds	1	tens	7	ones

____

6. Write the numeral.

3	hundreds	5	tens	6	ones

____

7. Write the numeral for two hundred seventy-two.

____

8. Write the numeral.

5	hundreds	8	tens	2	ones

____

Directions: Solve each problem.

1 How many sides does the shape have?  _______ sides

2 Color the square.

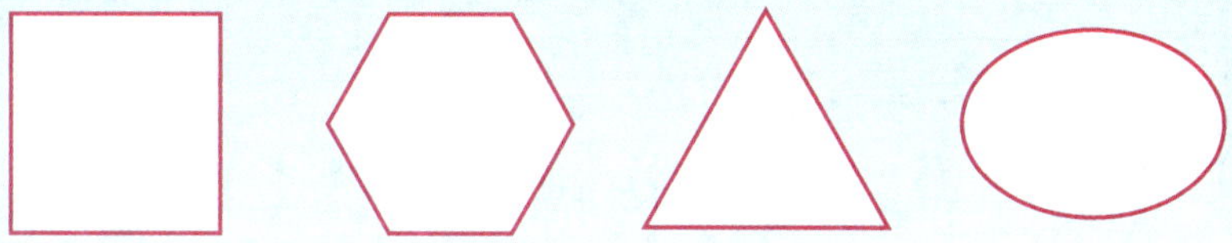

3 Circle the hexagon.

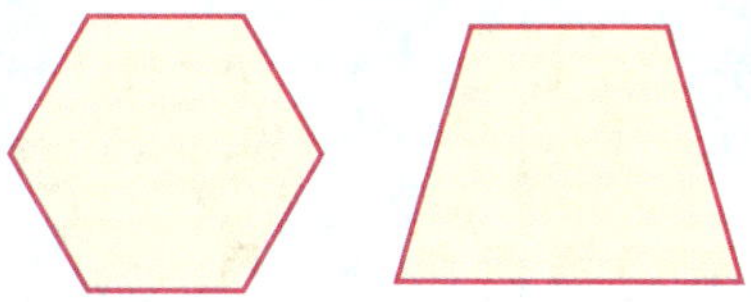

4 True or false? A hexagon has 7 angles. ________________

5 Color the shape with 3 sides.

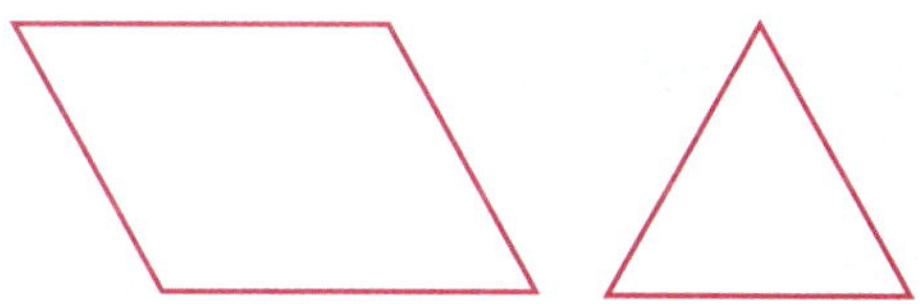

6 Draw the top view of the solid.

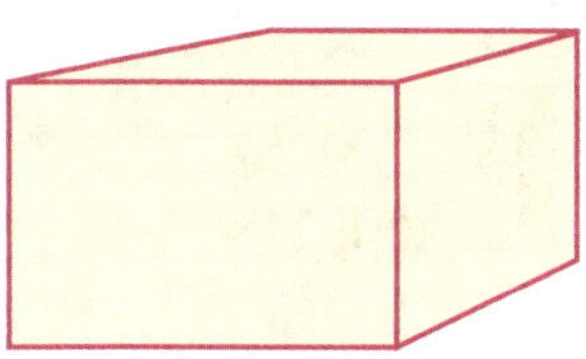

7 True or false? Rectangles have four vertices. _____________

Directions: Look at the example. Then, solve the problems.

Example: Look at the base-ten blocks. Write the number of hundreds, tens, and ones.

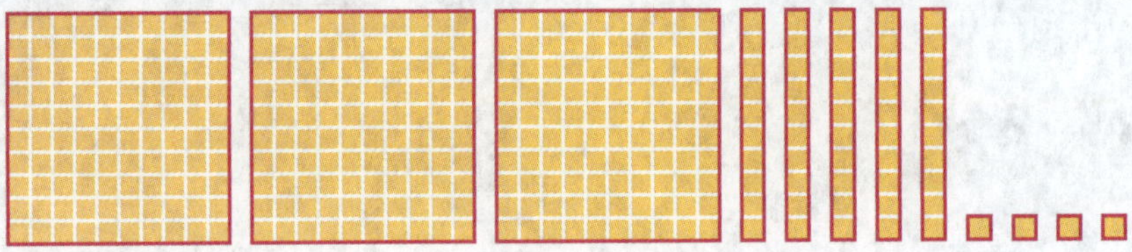

___3___ hundreds ___5___ tens ___4___ ones

The number is ___354___.

1. Look at the base-ten blocks. Write the number of hundreds, tens, and ones.

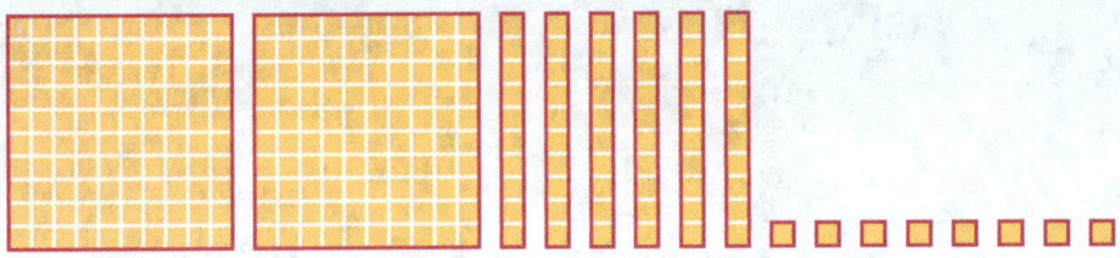

________ hundreds ________ tens ________ ones

The number is ________________.

2. Look at the base-ten blocks. Write the number of hundreds, tens, and ones.

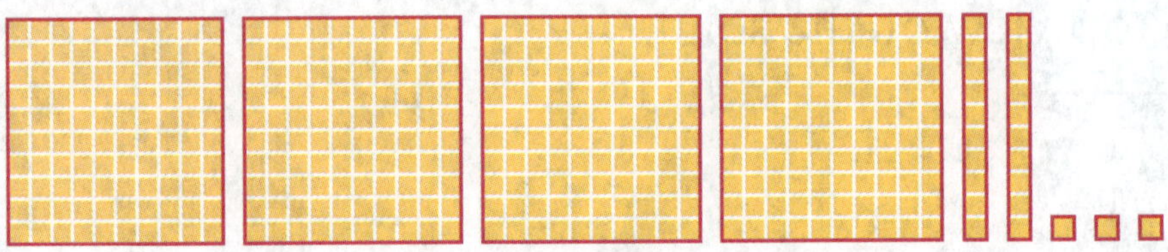

________ hundreds ________ tens ________ ones

The number is ________________.

Directions: Show two ways to solve the problem.

1. There are eight hundred forty-two students at Cleveland Elementary School. What are two ways to write this number?

Strategy 1

Expanded form:

________ + ________ + ________

Strategy 2

Number form:

____

2. How are the two strategies different?

____

____

____

____

____

____

Directions: Read the list of character traits. Circle the traits that are important for being a good leader. Then, answer the questions.

Character Traits

- honest
- fast runner
- hardworking
- caring
- funny
- dependable
- rich
- smart

1. List four leaders in your school or community.

_______________ _______________

_______________ _______________

2. What traits do these people have that make them good leaders?

____

3. How can you be a leader at home?

____

____

4. How can you be a leader with your friends?

____

____

Directions: Follow the steps in this experiment to closely examine pebbles.

What You Need

- 10 pebbles
- large, clear plastic jar
- magnifying glass
- water

What to Do

1. Use a magnifying glass to look closely at one pebble. Draw what you see.

2. Place all the pebbles in the plastic jar. Draw what you see.

3. Pour water over the pebbles. Draw what you see.

Pebbles in Jar	Pebbles in Water

4. What changed? What didn't change?

Directions: Every mini-grid must have each shape.
Every column must have each shape.
Every row must have each shape.

Directions: Play the game with two more people. Take turns rolling two number cubes. Match your roll to a word on the board. Write your initials in that row, and read the word aloud. If you roll 12, write your initials in any row. The first person to write his or her initials in all 10 rows wins.

Roll	Word	Player 1	Player 2	Player 3
2	keep			
3	house			
4	school			
5	people			
6	brother			
7	never			
8	morning			
9	tree			
10	climb			
11	father			

Mathematics Activity

Find different shapes while you're at home or in your community. Count the number of sides, and name each shape.

Problem-Solving Activity

Find numbers on signs, in books, and around your neighborhood. Write the numbers in expanded form, as words, and as numerals.

Social Studies Activity

Choose a leader from your school or community. Make a list of all the reasons that person is a good leader. Then, write and send a letter to the person explaining why he or she is a good leader.

Science Activity

Have an adult break apart some pebbles with a hammer. Use a magnifying glass to observe the insides of the pebbles. Write and draw your observations.

Critical-Thinking Activity

Make your own sudoku grid. Use four shapes to make the puzzle. Have a family member solve the puzzle. Hint: First, make a completed grid. Then, copy it, but leave out shapes from each row or column.

Listening-and-Speaking Activity

Interview a friend or family member. Ask his or her opinion about what makes a good leader.

Directions: Read the text, and answer the questions.

Max's Cars

Max loves his toy cars. Sometimes, he plays with them for hours. He has all different kinds of cars. Some of them are race cars, and others are trucks. He plays many different games with them. His friends like cars, too, so they trade cars with each other. Max prefers his cars to any other toy in the house.

1. What does Max like to play with more than his toy cars?
   - (A) clocks
   - (B) trucks
   - (C) games
   - (D) nothing

2. What is the main idea?
   - (A) Max has friends.
   - (B) Max likes race cars.
   - (C) Max loves his toy cars.
   - (D) Max trades cars.

3. Which word has the same root word as *preferred*?
   - (A) performed
   - (B) preference
   - (C) referred
   - (D) referee

4. Which of these words means *preferred*?
   - (A) asked
   - (B) favored
   - (C) chose
   - (D) decided

Directions: Read the text, and answer the questions.

Different Flags

There are many different kinds of flags. They are usually in the shape of a rectangle, but some are squares or triangles. A flag can be held, or it can be flown. Some flags are even twirled! Flags wave in the wind. They have all sorts of designs on them. People hang flags to show respect. They may want to honor a special day.

1. Which is the best new title for the text?
   - (A) "Flag Time"
   - (B) "Show Respect"
   - (C) "Flags for All Reasons"
   - (D) "Twirling"

2. According to this text, how are flags used?
   - (A) They are held.
   - (B) They are flown.
   - (C) They are twirled.
   - (D) all of the above

3. How many syllables are in the word *designs*?
   - (A) one syllable
   - (B) two syllables
   - (C) three syllables
   - (D) four syllables

4. What else is in the shape of a rectangle?
   - (A) a door
   - (B) a clock
   - (C) a pizza slice
   - (D) a cupcake

Directions: Read each set of words. Circle the word from the Word Bank. Then, use that word in a sentence.

Word Bank

• saw	• earth	• light	• thought	• under
• city	• eye	• head	• story	• start

1. light, long, right

    ____

    ____

2. eye, down, most

    ____

    ____

3. over, any, city

    ____

    ____

4. start, just, old

    ____

    ____

UNIT 3

Language

Directions: Fill in the bubble next to the correct answer.

1. Which shows a correct singular and plural?
   - Ⓐ one car/two cars
   - Ⓑ one table/two table
   - Ⓒ one cats/two cats

2. What would you call a large number of flowers?
   - Ⓐ a group of flowers
   - Ⓑ a bouquet of flowers
   - Ⓒ a herd of flowers

3. Many plural nouns end in *–s* or *–es*. Which noun does not follow this rule?
   - Ⓐ toe
   - Ⓑ finger
   - Ⓒ foot

4. What would you call a large amount of ants?
   - Ⓐ an army of ants
   - Ⓑ a herd of ants
   - Ⓒ a flock of ants

5. Many plural nouns end in *–s* or *–es*. Which noun does not follow this rule?
   - Ⓐ sheep
   - Ⓑ hat
   - Ⓒ adult

6. Many plural nouns end in *–s* or *–es*. Which noun does not follow this rule?
   - Ⓐ cat
   - Ⓑ table
   - Ⓒ man

7. Which shows a correct singular and plural?
   - Ⓐ foot/foots
   - Ⓑ child/children
   - Ⓒ fish/fishs

8. What would you call a group of islands?
   - Ⓐ a chain of islands
   - Ⓑ a herd of islands
   - Ⓒ a flock of islands

Directions: Think about what happens during a bad day. Write two things in each box that might make a day feel bad.

When you get up, …

____________________ ____________________

When you arrive at school, …

____________________ ____________________

At lunch, …

____________________ ____________________

After school, …

____________________ ____________________

In the evening, …

____________________ ____________________

Directions: Have you ever had a bad day? Describe what happened and what you did to make the day better. Draw a picture to go with your narrative. Use your notes on page 41 to help you.

Remember!

A strong narrative:

- tells a story
- has a beginning, a middle, and an end
- includes descriptive details

Directions: Solve each problem.

1. Circle the object that is shorter than 1 meter in height.

2. Circle the object that would be taller than 1 meter.

3. Is an elephant taller or shorter than 1 yard?

____

4. Circle the best estimate for the height.

   10 meters   2 meters

5. Circle the object that is shorter than 1 meter.

6. Is a door less than 1 meter or more than 1 meter?

____

7. Circle the best estimate.

   1 meter   5 meters

Directions: Solve each problem.

1. Write the time shown.

half past ___________

2. Write the time.

3. Write the time shown.

half past ___________

4. Show 1:00.

5. Show 4:30.

6. Write the time.

7. Write the time.

8. Show 7:30.

Directions: Read and solve the problem.

Mr. Rios has two cows on his farm. One cow weighs 732 pounds. Another cow weighs 832 pounds. Compare the weights using >, <, or =.

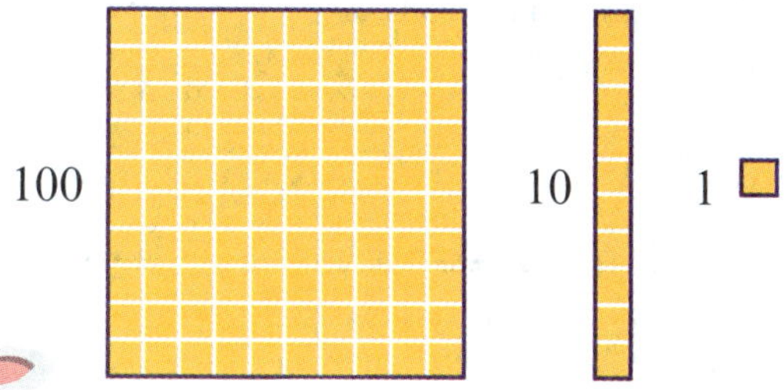

1. What do you know about the problem?

____

____

2. What do you need to find?

____

____

3. How many hundreds, tens, and ones are in 732 and 832?

732 = ________ hundreds ________ tens ________ ones

832 = ________ hundreds ________ tens ________ ones

4. 732 ◯ 832

Directions: Read and solve the problem.

Problem: Mr. Andrews has two cows on his farm. One cow weighs 951 pounds. Another cow weighs 915 pounds. Compare the weights using >, <, or =.

List What You Know	Make a Plan
Solve the Problem	**Look Back and Explain**
______ ☐ ______	

Directions: Draw a map of your neighborhood in the grid below. Use symbols to show your home, stores, and parks. Label your symbols in the key.

Map Key

Directions: Check the moon once a week for four weeks. Draw it each week.

Week 1	Week 2
Week 3	Week 4

What conclusions can you draw?

____

____

____

____

Directions: Create a secret code with numbers or symbols. Assign one number or symbol to each letter of the alphabet. Then, use your code to write a secret message.

A	B	C	D	E	F	G	H	I	J	K	L	M
N	**O**	**P**	**Q**	**R**	**S**	**T**	**U**	**V**	**W**	**X**	**Y**	**Z**

Your Message

Directions: Play the game with a partner. Each player should place a small object at the start. Take turns rolling a number cube. Move your object the number of spaces that you roll. In the space that you land, tell which punctuation mark (. ? !) completes the sentence. If you are correct, stay on that space. If you answer incorrectly, move back one space. The first player to reach the finish line wins.

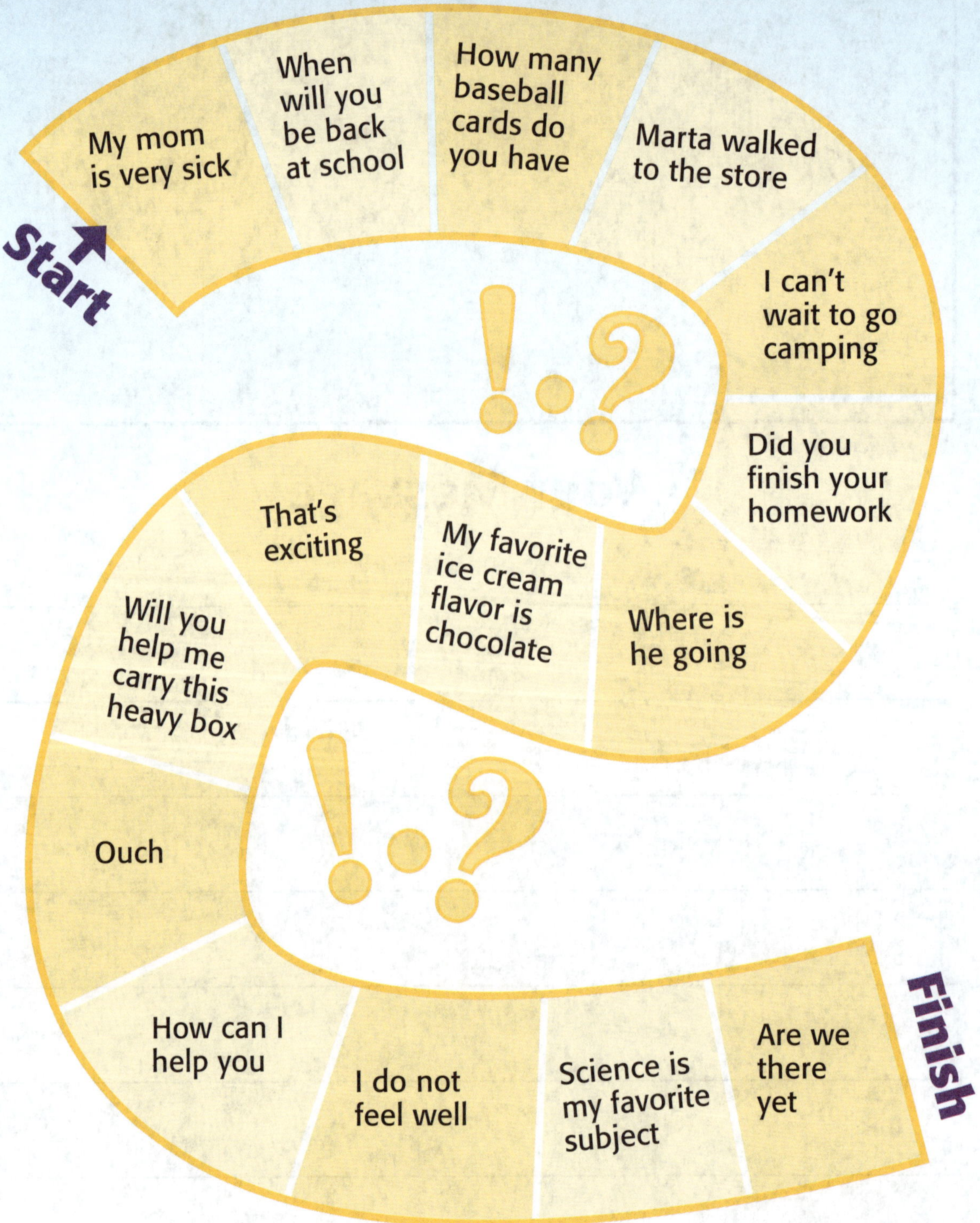

High-Frequency Words Activity

Use magnetic letters or letter tiles to create each word from the Word Bank on page 39. Read each word aloud.

Mathematics Activity

Choose five items from your home. Estimate the length of each item. Then, use a ruler or a tape measure to find the actual length of each item.

Problem-Solving Activity

Look for numbers around your home or neighborhood. Compare the numbers to determine which are greater.

Social Studies Activity

Draw and label a map of your bedroom. Be sure to include doors, windows, and furniture. Use a key to describe any symbols you use.

Critical-Thinking Activity

Give your code from page 49 to a family member. Ask him or her to write a sentence with your code. Then, decode the sentence.

Listening-and-Speaking Activity

Choose a favorite animal. Record yourself discussing at least two facts about that animal. Use at least two adjectives to describe the animal.

Directions: Read the text, and answer the questions.

An Amazing Day at the Beach

The young girl walked on the beach. She noticed something moving in the water. But she was not sure what it was. Could it be a dolphin, a shark, or a whale? It had an interesting fin. She kept her eye on the same spot. Then, from the water emerged the head of a beautiful girl. She realized something amazing. She had just seen a mermaid!

1. What happened right after the girl saw the fin?
   - (A) She knew it was a mermaid.
   - (B) She saw a head.
   - (C) She kept her eye on the same spot.
   - (D) She screamed.

2. How do you know the text is fantasy?
   - (A) Young girls don't walk on the beach alone.
   - (B) Mermaids are not real.
   - (C) Mermaids are not girls.
   - (D) Sharks and whales eat mermaids.

3. How many syllables are in the word *amazing*?
   - (A) one syllable
   - (B) two syllables
   - (C) three syllables
   - (D) four syllables

4. Which word means *realized*?
   - (A) mentioned
   - (B) found
   - (C) breathed
   - (D) understood

Directions: Read the text, and answer the questions.

The Olympic Games

The Olympic Games are a sporting event. They happen every two years. Athletes compete from around the world. They compete for medals. There are summer games and winter games. The athletes are the best in their sports. People all over the world like to watch. They root for their countries!

1. What is the main topic?
   - (A) sports
   - (B) the Olympic Games
   - (C) athletes
   - (D) summer and winter games

2. Which does NOT describe the Olympic Games?
   - (A) a sporting event in summer and winter
   - (B) a sporting event with countries competing against one another
   - (C) a sporting event that no one watches
   - (D) a sporting event with medals for the winners

3. Which word has the same root word as *sporting*?
   - (A) snorting
   - (B) sports
   - (C) chatting
   - (D) port

4. Which word means *to try to win*?
   - (A) watch
   - (B) root
   - (C) compete
   - (D) happen

Directions: Unscramble each word. Use the Word Bank to help you.

Word Bank

- left
- few
- along
- fast
- with
- next
- while
- slow
- them
- how

1. sfta ____________________
2. wef ____________________
3. owh ____________________
4. nalog ____________________
5. olsw ____________________
6. tihw ____________________
7. tlfe ____________________
8. ilweh ____________________
9. tnxe ____________________
10. mhte ____________________

Directions: Read and answer each question.

1. Rewrite the sentence using an apostrophe.

   The pool belonging to Mario felt very refreshing on a hot day.

   ____

   ____

2. Add apostrophes to the sentence.

   Drivers dont always know when a cars gas is almost out.

3. Add apostrophes to the following contractions.

   doesnt wont havent

4. Circle the contraction in the sentence.

   The students should've studied harder for the challenging test.

5. Use an apostrophe to write *the petal on the flower* in another way.

   ____

UNIT 4

Writing

Directions: List at least three ideas in each column.

The Beach

What I Like	What I Don't Like

The Park

What I Like	What I Don't Like

Directions: Do you prefer the beach or the park? Explain why, using strong supporting details. Draw a picture to support your opinion. Use your notes on page 56 to help you.

Remember!

An opinion paragraph includes:

- an introductory sentence that states your opinion
- details to support your ideas
- a concluding sentence

Directions: Solve each problem.

1. Who checked out the most library books during the second week?

   ____

Library Books Checked Out

	Week 1	Week 2	Week 3
Joey	4	5	5
Emily	4	4	4
Brenda	5	7	6
Allison	6	3	6

3. How many trains were sold on the weekdays?

   ____

Toy Train Sales Last week

2. Who caught the fewest fish?

   ____

Fish Caught

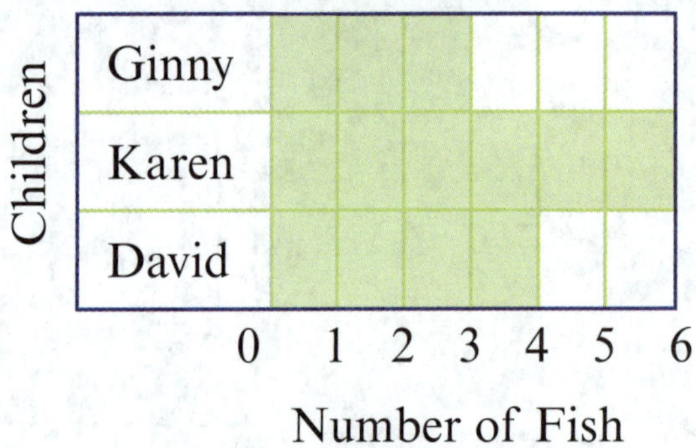

4. Which children do not play soccer?

   ____

Sports Played

	Soccer	Swimming	Volleyball
Mark	X		X
Tracy		X	
Mike		X	X

Directions: Solve each subtraction problem. The first one is done for you.

1.  6 − 1 = 5

2.  ☐ − ☐ = ☐

3.  ☐ − ☐ = ☐

4.  ☐ − ☐ = ☐

5.  ☐ − ☐ = ☐

6.  ☐ − ☐ = ☐

7.  ☐ − ☐ = ☐

8.  ☐ − ☐ = ☐

Directions: Look at the example. Then, solve the problem using a number line.

Example: Jasper has 16 red marbles and 5 purple marbles. How many marbles does he have in all? Write a number sentence to show the answer, and show your work on the number line.

16 + 5 = 21

1. Jessica has 12 red marbles and 7 purple marbles. How many marbles does she have in all? Write a number sentence to show the answer, and show your work on the number line.

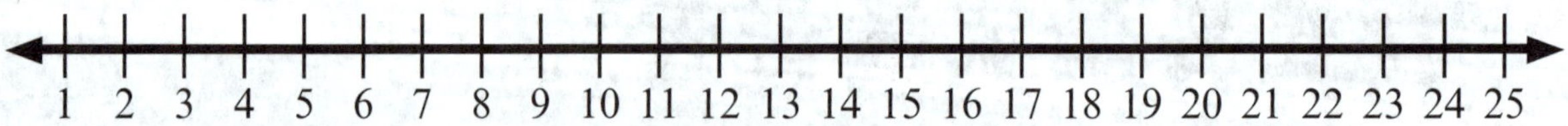

____

2. She buys 5 white marbles. How many marbles does she have in all now? Write a number sentence to show the answer. Show your work on the number line above.

____

Directions: Show two ways to solve the problem.

1. Sophia has 26 red crayons. She has 12 blue crayons. How many crayons does Sophia have altogether?

Strategy 1: Use the ten frames to solve the problem.

○	○	○	○	○
○	○	○	○	○

○	○	○	○	○
○	○	○	○	○

○	○	○	○	○
○	○	○	○	○

○	○	○	○	○
○	○	○	○	○

Strategy 2: Start with 26 and count on to solve the problem.

26 ________ ________ ________ ________

________ ________ ________ ________

________ ________ ________ ________

2. Which strategy do you think is easier? Explain your reasoning.

____

____

UNIT 4

Social Studies

Directions: Match each person in the first column with his or her responsibility in the second column. Hint: Some people may have more than one responsibility.

teacher	keep the community safe
child	respond to emergencies
parent	provide food, shelter, and clothing
police officer	do homework
firefighter	keep students safe
principal	provide customer service
store clerk	keep people healthy
doctor	drive people around the city
nurse	keep bedroom clean
bus driver	put out fires

Write about one thing you are responsible for doing at home.

____

____

____

____

____

Directions: Follow the steps in this experiment to discover how seeds are different.

What You Need

- many different seeds
- jar with lid

What to Do

1. Put all the seeds in a jar.
2. Choose a seed. Take it out, and look at it carefully.
3. Draw a picture of your seed.

4. Put the seed back in the jar. Shake the seeds around.
5. Try to find your seed again. How do you know it's the same seed?

____

____

____

Directions: Look at each puzzle. Write the word or phrase that each puzzle represents.

1 BAD wolf ______	4 s t a n d me ______
2 SH get APE ______	5 SLOW ______
3 PROMISE ______	6 stood MISS ______

Directions: Take turns rolling two number cubes with a partner. After each roll, add the numbers on the cubes. Match the sum to the word in the chart, and add a tally mark next to it. Read the word in a robot voice. Keep rolling until you have each rolled 20 times.

Roll	Word	Tallies
2	left	
3	next	
4	few	
5	while	
6	along	
7	slow	
8	fast	
9	them	
10	with	
11	how	
12	robot	

1. Which word(s) did you roll the most?

____

2. Which word(s) did you roll the least?

____

Writing Activity

Write a paragraph about your least favorite place to visit. Include reasons why you don't like it and why other people should not visit this place.

Mathematics Activity

Ask your family and friends about their favorite ice cream flavors. Use their answers to create a bar graph that shows how many people like each flavor.

Social Studies Activity

Make a list of ways that you can be responsible at home. Ask your parents to review the list to see if there are any responsibilities they want you to add. Post the list in your home to remind you of the things you need to do to be responsible.

Science Activity

Plant several different seeds in separate containers of soil. Give them a little water each day. Observe them as they begin to grow. How are the plants alike? How are they different?

Critical-Thinking Activity

Create your own word puzzle. Have a friend or a family member solve your puzzle.

Listening-and-Speaking Activity

Tell your family about your favorite sport or game. Be sure to include at least two reasons to support your opinion about why it is your favorite.

Directions: Read the text, and answer the questions.

Acting Strange

Jesse walked down the street and kept his eyes on the ground. "What are you doing, Jesse?" his mom asked. She was perplexed. Jesse kept hopping over something.

"I'm trying to avoid the cracks, Mom," said Jesse. He was trying not to step on each crack in the sidewalk, and it was difficult. He thought something bad might happen if he stepped on a crack. He was being superstitious.

1. Why is Jesse keeping his eyes on the ground?
   - (A) He does not want to talk to his mom.
   - (B) He is looking for cracks in the sidewalk.
   - (C) He is looking for insects to step on.
   - (D) He is trying to be good.

2. Why is Jesse avoiding sidewalk cracks?
   - (A) He thinks something bad might happen.
   - (B) He likes to hop.
   - (C) He is frustrated with his mom.
   - (D) He cannot see them.

3. Which root word with an *–ed* ending is not in the text?
   - (A) walk
   - (B) perplex
   - (C) step
   - (D) work

4. What is an example of being superstitious?
   - (A) wearing a bicycle helmet
   - (B) never choosing unlucky number 13
   - (C) not watching television for a week
   - (D) walking backwards out of a room

Directions: Read the text, and answer the questions.

Dinosaurs

Dinosaurs used to roam Earth. Now, they are gone. We do not know for sure where they went or what happened to them. Scientists have theories. Some say an asteroid hit Earth, while others think a disease spread among the dinosaurs. An ice age may have started it all. We may never know for sure what happened.

1. What is the main idea of this text?
   - (A) Scientists develop theories.
   - (B) The reason dinosaurs are gone is a mystery.
   - (C) Asteroids hit Earth.
   - (D) An ice age may have happened.

2. Which idea is NOT suggested as a reason why dinosaurs are gone?
   - (A) a disease
   - (B) an asteroid
   - (C) an ice age
   - (D) a volcanic eruption

3. What is the root word in *started*?
   - (A) tart
   - (B) start
   - (C) ted
   - (D) art

4. Which word is a synonym for *roam*?
   - (A) destroy
   - (B) attack
   - (C) rule
   - (D) travel

Directions: Write the correct word from the Word Bank to complete each sentence. Then, write your own sentence using one of the words.

Word Bank

• hard	• example	• life	• those	• paper
• open	• begin	• always	• both	• together

1. The jar was ________________ to open.
2. The movie will ________________ in ten minutes.
3. I have lived in the country my whole ________________.
4. The gate to the backyard was left ________________.
5. I followed the ________________ in the directions.
6. The ________________ is on the desk.
7. ________________ eat a healthy breakfast.
8. I think ________________ of these puppies are cute.
9. Can I have some of ________________ yummy cookies?
10. He likes to mix paint colors ________________.

____

____

Directions: Answer each question.

1. Complete the sentence with a noun and an adverb.

   A swarm of ________________ moved ________________.

2. Write a sentence using the adjective *young*.

   ____

   ____

3. Circle the adverbs in the sentence.

   Kara lovingly hugged her brother before he quickly walked to the bus stop.

4. Write a sentence using the word *bunch* to describe several objects.

   ____

   ____

5. Complete the sentence with a noun and an adverb.

   A litter of ________________ ran ________________.

6. Complete the sentence with a noun and an adverb.

   A choir of ________________ sang ________________.

Directions: Circle the turtles with information that could be included in an informative/explanatory paragraph about turtles.

Turtles are reptiles.

Turtles are rather strange looking.

Turtles lay eggs.

My brother likes turtles.

Some turtles live on land and others in water.

Turtles have upper and lower shells.

Turtle shells have different designs.

Turtles are cold blooded.

Directions: Write an informative/explanatory paragraph about turtles. Draw a picture to support your writing. Use the notes from page 71 to help you.

Remember!

A strong informative/explanatory paragraph should:

- include only relevant information
- have an introductory and a concluding sentence
- use details to support the topic

Directions: Solve each problem.

1. Cami has 23 shells in her collection. How many shells will she have if she doubles her collection?

   ____

2. A survey was taken to see which places kids like best. There were 67 kids who liked the beach. There were 99 kids who liked the aquarium. There were 46 kids who liked the zoo. How many more kids liked the beach than the zoo?

   ____

3. Kristy has a sticker collection with 23 glitter stickers, 56 puffy stickers, and 14 scratch-n-sniff stickers. If she gets 16 more glitter stickers, how many glitter stickers will she have in all?

   ____

4. Pearl scored 23 points in the game she was playing. Then, she scored 42 more points. How many points did she score altogether?

   ____

5. A survey was taken by the cafeteria manager. It showed that 83 children like pizza and 57 like spaghetti. How many more children like pizza than spaghetti?

   ____

6. Twila has 6 toy ponies, 5 toy puppies, and 7 toy kitties. How many toy animals does she have in all?

   ____

Directions: Solve each problem.

1. What is 35¢ more than 3 dimes and 2 nickels?

   ____

2. You have 34 trading cards. You win 15 more in a game. Then, you lose 12. How many trading cards do you have now?

   ____

3. Jack has 15 quarters, 3 dimes, and 7 pennies. If he gets 6 more dimes, how many dimes will he have?

   ____

4. Tina wants to buy a doll that costs $13.00. She gets $2.00 every week in her allowance. How many weeks will she have to save her allowance so she can buy the doll?

   ____

5. What is 12¢ less than 2 quarters?

   ____

6. Brady gets 25¢ each day in allowance. How much money does he get each week?

   ____

7. A banana costs 19¢, an apple costs 26¢, and a pear costs 35¢. Rita has 65¢. Can she buy all three pieces of fruit?

   ____

8. You have 62¢ in your piggy bank. Your mom gives you a quarter and a dime. You spend 35¢. How much money do you have left?

   ____

Directions: Read and solve the problem.

Olivia scores 89 points in a video game. She plays another game and scores 57 points. What is the difference between the points she scores on the two games?

1. What do you know about the problem?

____

____

2. What do you need to find?

____

____

3. How can you solve the problem?

____

____

4. What is the difference between the points she scores on the two games?

____

____

Directions: Read and solve the problem.

Problem: Jason scores 94 points in a video game. He plays another game and scores 72 points. What is the difference between the points he scores on the two games?

List What You Know	Make a Plan
Solve the Problem	**Look Back and Explain**

Directions: Mark where you live on the map. Be as exact as you can. Then, answer the questions.

1. What is the name of your country?

____

2. What is the name of your city or town?

____

3. What is your address?

____

____

____

4. Where would you like to visit someday?

____

____

Directions: Follow the steps in this experiment to discover what is inside leaves.

What You Need

- large plastic container
- small stone
- fresh leaves
- small plastic container
- plastic sheeting
- magnifying glass

What to Do

1. Gather enough leaves to fill the large container halfway.
2. Place the small container inside the large one. Arrange the leaves around the small container.
3. Cover the top with plastic sheeting.
4. Place the stone on top of the plastic sheeting. Center it over the small container.
5. Place the container outside in the sun for five days.
6. After five days, carefully remove the plastic sheeting. Observe the containers. Describe what you see.

____

____

____

Directions: Solve each clue. Each answer starts with the letter *m*.

Clue	Word that starts with *m*
1 a zoo animal that eats bananas	
2 a type of baked breakfast food	
3 a type of insect that bites people's skin	
4 to heat something and make it a liquid	
5 a synonym for *angry*	
6 to make something larger so you can see it	
7 an antonym for *clean* or *neat*	
8 a large, grassy area	

Directions: Work with a partner. Take turns rolling a number cube. Each number on the cube represents an amount of money. After you have both rolled, draw the money that your rolls represent. After you have each rolled five times, find the total amount of money.

Key

Roll 1

Roll 2

Roll 3

Roll 4

Roll 5

Total amount of money: ____________________

High-Frequency Words Activity

Put some finger paint inside a plastic zipper bag. Seal the bag. On the outside of the bag, use your finger to write one word from the Word Bank on page 69. Smooth the paint to erase the word, and write the next word. Repeat for each word.

Mathematics Activity

Ask a family member to give you a collection of coins and bills. Count the total amount of money. Then, write a word problem that reflects the total amount of money you were given.

Social Studies Activity

Work with an adult to find where you live on a map. Mark your location on the map. Then, mark the locations of places you have visited with your family. You can even do this online or on a phone!

Critical-Thinking Activity

Choose a letter, and write your own riddle clues for words that start with that letter. Read your clues to someone. Ask that person to solve your riddles.

Listening-and-Speaking Activity

When talking with your family, try to use all the words from the Word Bank on page 69. Find creative ways to add these words to the conversations.

Directions: Read the text, and answer the questions on the next page.

Johnny Appleseed

Johnny Appleseed lived long ago. He was born in 1774. His real name was John Chapman. He was famous for planting apple trees.

Some stories claim that he just spread seeds around. But Johnny knew a lot about trees. He knew where they should grow. He set up nurseries. These are places for trees to grow. The trees were sold to people. Then, people planted the trees on their land. Johnny wanted apple trees to grow over large areas of land. He wanted to protect things in nature.

This story has been passed down over the years. Some facts are true. Some facts have been exaggerated. It is a folktale that many people know.

One reason Johnny Appleseed is famous is because he was a warm and kind man. He treated others well. He lived a simple life. Johnny cared deeply about animals. He looked after things in nature. He is a hero. He is admired for his good nature and his good deeds.

Directions: Read "Johnny Appleseed," and then answer the questions.

1. Who might make the strongest connection to the text?
   - Ⓐ a little girl who does not like to eat apples
   - Ⓑ a teacher who likes to read
   - Ⓒ a young boy who goes to the beach
   - Ⓓ a man who plants seeds in his garden

2. What kind of story is "Johnny Appleseed"?
   - Ⓐ a foketale
   - Ⓑ a folktale
   - Ⓒ a fulltale
   - Ⓓ a folktall

3. What is a hero?
   - Ⓐ a strong person
   - Ⓑ a person who lives a simple life
   - Ⓒ a person who is admired by others
   - Ⓓ a person who lived long ago

4. Where did Johnny Appleseed get his nickname?
   - Ⓐ He planted apple trees and protected nature.
   - Ⓑ He bought and sold apples.
   - Ⓒ He baked apple pies.
   - Ⓓ He was good to animals and people.

5. Which gives the best summary?
   - Ⓐ Johnny Appleseed is a famous farmer.
   - Ⓑ Johnny Appleseed's story is a folktale many people know.
   - Ⓒ Johnny Appleseed invented the apple.
   - Ⓓ Johnny Appleseed knew a lot about trees.

Directions: Write each word. Then, write each word backward.

1. got

2. group

3. often

4. run

5. important

6. children

7. side

8. car

9. feet

10. until

Directions: Answer each question.

1. Add commas to this letter.

   Dear Coach

   I learned a lot about soccer from you.

   Your player

   Romeo

2. Write a closing for the letter.

   Dear City Council,

   I would like to request that Johnson Park stay open.

   Closing this park would make many people very sad, including me.

   ____

   ____

   ____

3. Add commas to the letter.

   Dear Dad

   I am very sorry that I lost your keys.

   I will help you find them.

   Your son

   Pablo

4. Add commas to the letter.

   Dear Luis

   Will you come to my party? It is on Saturday.

   Your friend

   Sam

Directions: In the middle apple, circle your favorite way to eat apples. In the outer apples, write four reasons why you like eating apples that way.

I like eating apple slices.

I like eating apples with caramel sauce.

I like eating apple pie.

I like eating applesauce.

Directions: Describe the best way to eat apples. Include reasons to support your opinion. Use your notes on page 86 to help you.

Edit and Revise!

Be sure that you check your writing for:

- capital letters at the beginning of sentences
- capitalized proper nouns
- reasons that support your opinion

Directions: Solve each problem.

1.
$$\begin{array}{r} 64 \\ +\ 22 \\ \hline \end{array}$$

2. 27 – 16 = ________

3.
$$\begin{array}{r} 45 \\ +\ 73 \\ \hline \end{array}$$

4. 60 – 38 = ________

5. 72 plus 27 equals

____

6. 78 – 63 = ________

7.
$$\begin{array}{r} 82 \\ -\ 66 \\ \hline \end{array}$$

8. 47 + 46 = ________

9.
$$\begin{array}{r} 61 \\ +\ 35 \\ \hline \end{array}$$

10. 85 – 22 = ________

11. 18 plus 56 equals

____

12. 31 minus 24 equals

____

Directions: Solve each problem.

1. Count the angles. ________

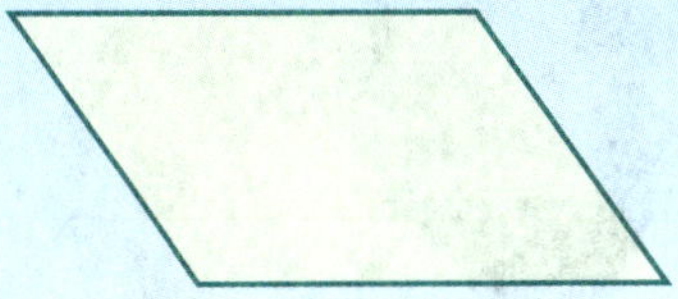

2. True or false?
A solid shape is a two-dimensional object.

____

3. Color the trapezoid.

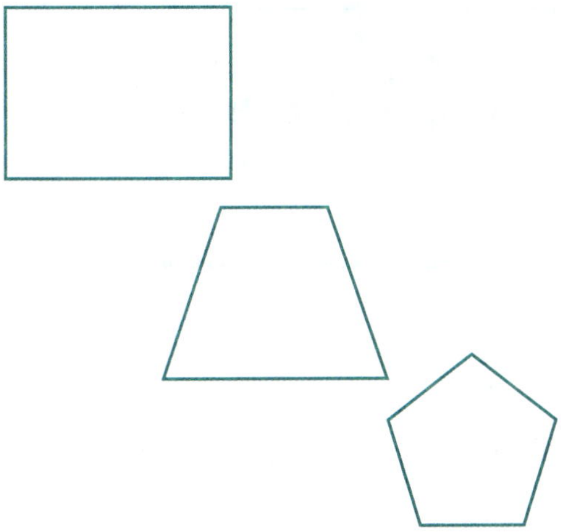

4. Name the shape.

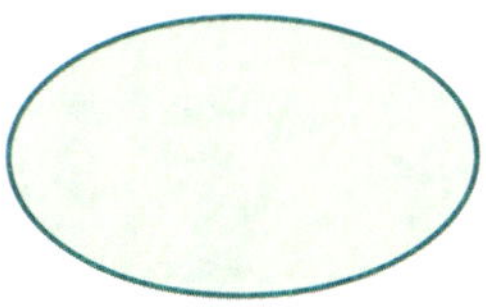

5. Color the polygon with 3 sides.

6. Count the angles. ________

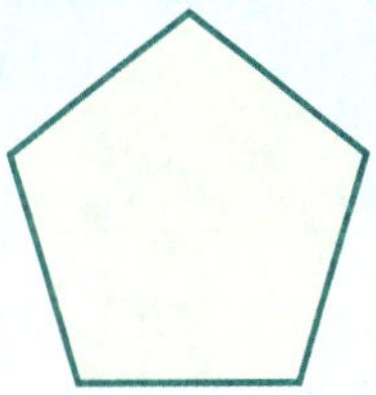

7. Name the solid.

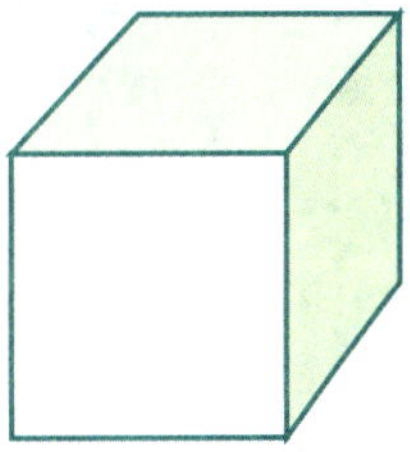

____

8. Name the shape.

____

Directions: Read and solve the problem.

A lion can run 54 miles per hour. It runs 12 miles per hour faster than a coyote. What is the combined speed of the lion and the coyote?

1. Write a number sentence to show how fast a coyote can run.

____

2. Write a number sentence to show the combined speed of the lion and the coyote.

____

3. Show how you found the combined speed of the lion and the coyote.

Directions: Read and solve the problem.

Students in three second-grade classes are going on a field trip. There is a total of 88 students. Use six of the numbers in the squares to write an addition sentence that tells about the problem. You may use the numbers more than once.

0	1	2	3	4	5	6	7	8	9

1. What number sentence can you write?

☐☐ + ☐☐ + ☐☐ = 88

2. Show your work to prove your number sentence is true.

Directions: Use a dictionary to look up the definition of the word *justice*. Then, write an acrostic poem that gives examples of justice.

J ______________________________

U ______________________________

S ______________________________

T ______________________________

I ______________________________

C ______________________________

E ______________________________

Directions: Follow the steps in this experiment to discover what is in your square meter.

What You Need

- ruler
- pegs
- string
- thermometer
- notebook

What to Do

1. Go outside, and find a place with some vegetation.
2. Use the ruler to accurately measure one square meter.
3. Push one peg into each corner of the square meter. Tie string around the pegs to mark the perimeter.
4. Write your observations in your notebook. Record the date, the temperature, weather conditions, each type of plant, and each type of insect.
5. In your notebook, draw a detailed diagram of your square, and label each thing you see. Include a key for each type of plant and insect.
6. Revisit your square meter for the next three days. If you can, observe at different times of the day. In your notebook, record what has changed and what has stayed the same.
7. Summarize your results in your notebook.

Directions: Look at the shape below. Find as many triangles as you can in the shape. Outline each triangle, and then write the total number.

There are ______________________ triangles.

Directions: Remove the face cards and aces from a deck of cards. Then, shuffle the remaining cards. Play with a partner. Take turns turning over two cards. Write a number sentence to add the numbers on the cards. Then, write whether the total is an odd or an even number. The person with the most odd totals wins.

Number Sentence	Odd or Even?
Example: 3 + 10 = 13	odd

High-Frequency Words Activity

Bounce a ball as you spell each word from page 84. For example, bounce the ball five times as you say the letters in the word *until*.

Mathematics Activity

Use construction paper to cut out a square and a rectangle. Fold each shape in different ways. What other shapes can you make by folding them?

Problem-Solving Activity

Write number sentences for pairs of numbers. Then, write word problems that can be solved using your number sentences.

Social Studies Activity

Draw a picture that shows what *justice* means to you. Then, write a short paragraph to explain your thoughts.

Critical-Thinking Activity

Draw a square that contains several squares, like the triangles activity on page 94. Then, decide how many total squares are in the picture.

Listening-and-Speaking Activity

Read your paragraph about justice (see the social studies activity above) to your family. Then, have the listeners share their ideas about justice.

Directions: Read the text, and answer the questions on the next page.

No More Bullying

Two girls followed Sam home from school. He was walking by himself because his brother was home sick. He could hear the girls giggling and saying rude things behind him. It felt like they were getting closer and closer.

Sam did not understand why the girls were teasing him. He barely knew them, though one of the girls lived around the corner. Sam even thought she might be friends with his brother. Why was she being so mean to him?

Sam started to walk quickly as he rounded the corner to his street. His house was only five houses away. He could see his mailbox and his driveway. He began to jog.

The girls jogged after him, but then, Sam surprised them when he suddenly stopped running and turned around. "Why are you following me?" he yelled. "I don't like it, and I think you are bullying me."

The girls stopped in their tracks. "Bullying?" one asked. "No, we aren't. We are just having fun."

"I don't think it's funny," said Sam. "Please stop and leave me alone!"

"Okay, sorry, Sam," the girls muttered. They looked sad, but Sam was glad. He had taught them a lesson. What might seem fun can make someone else uncomfortable, and that is not okay. Sam walked into his house, hoping they would not bother him, or anyone else, again.

Directions: Read "No More Bullying," and then answer the questions.

1. Who might make the strongest connection to the text?
   - (A) any younger brother
   - (B) a person who has been bullied
   - (C) any boy
   - (D) people who like to swim

2. What does Sam do as he gets near home?
   - (A) jig
   - (B) jag
   - (C) jog
   - (D) jug

3. What does it mean to make someone *uncomfortable*?
   - (A) make someone yell
   - (B) make someone walk fast
   - (C) make someone feel sad
   - (D) make someone feel uneasy

4. What is the problem?
   - (A) Sam's brother is sick.
   - (B) Sam is angry.
   - (C) Sam is bothered by the girls.
   - (D) Sam gets lost walking home.

5. Which gives the best summary of the text?
   - (A) Sam is followed and teased on his way home.
   - (B) Sam stands up to his bullies on his way home.
   - (C) Sam walks home alone.
   - (D) Sam yells at some other kids.

Directions: Work with a partner. Take turns rolling two number cubes. Match the sum of the cubes to a word, and read it in a funny voice. Place a tally in the column next to it. If the sum is 12, mark and say all the words. Continue until you have read each word at least three times.

Number	Word	Tallies
2	four	
3	began	
4	river	
5	took	
6	grow	
7	listen	
8	went	
9	clock	
10	write	
11	caught	

Which word did you roll the most? ______________________________

UNIT 7

Language

Directions: Answer each question.

1. Write an adjective that makes sense in the sentence.

   The ____________________ waves crashed loudly.

2. Circle the adjectives in the sentence.

   The happy man smiled at his young child.

3. Circle the adjectives in the sentence.

   The lifelong friends watched the intense game.

4. Write an adjective that makes sense in the sentence.

   The ____________________ gift at my party was my favorite.

5. Write an adjective that makes sense in the sentence.

   I chose the ____________________ shirt to wear to school.

6. Circle the adjectives in the sentence.

   The surprise party was a fun event.

Directions: Brainstorm objects that can be pushed or pulled. An example is provided.

Directions: Describe how objects are pushed or pulled. Include differences between pulling and pushing. Use your notes on page 101 to help you.

Edit and Revise!

Be sure that you check your writing for:

- capital letters at the beginning of sentences
- capitalized proper nouns
- subject/verb agreement

Directions: Solve each problem.

1. Write the length.

_______ inches

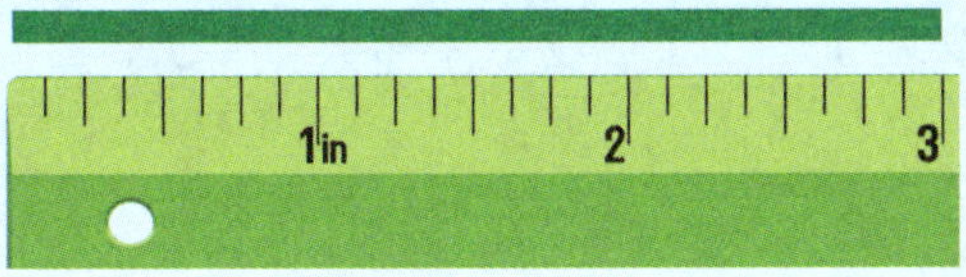

2. What tool would you use to measure length?

   (A) ruler

   (B) scale

   (C) clock

3. Circle the shorter row.

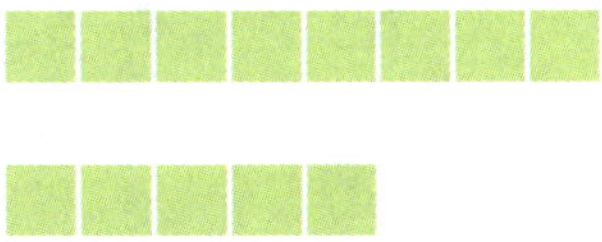

4. Circle the longer row.

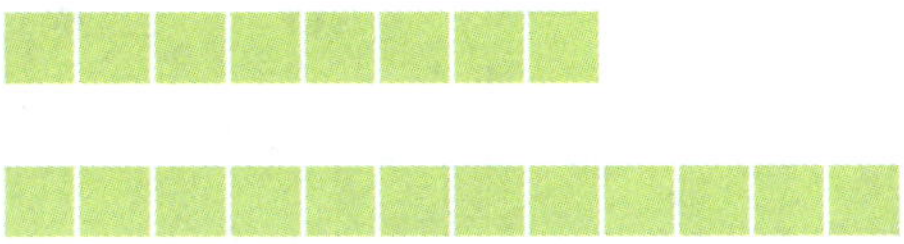

5. Write the length.

_______ centimeters

6. Write the length.

_______ inches

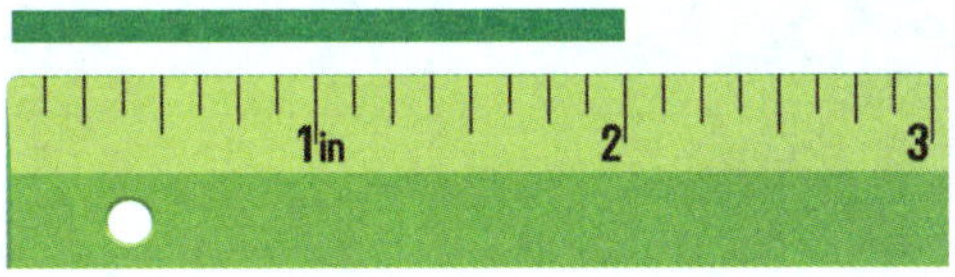

7. Circle the longer snake.

8. Write the length.

_______ centimeters

Directions: Solve each problem.

1. Use >, <, or =.

   125 ☐ 152

2. Order the numbers from smallest to largest.

   450 405 504

   ______ ______ ______

3. Order the numbers from largest to smallest.

   321 231 234

   ______ ______ ______

4. Use >, <, or =.

   987 ☐ 783

5. Order the numbers from largest to smallest.

   756 75 675

   ______ ______ ______

6. Use >, <, or =.

   377 ☐ 377

7. Order the numbers from smallest to largest.

   823 832 820

   ______ ______ ______

8. Use >, <, or =.

   399 ☐ 499

Directions: Read and solve the problem.

Kelly arranges 24 crackers on a platter. How can she arrange the crackers in equal rows? Make four different arrays. Write an addition sentence for each array.

______________________	______________________
______________________	______________________

UNIT 7

Problem Solving

Directions: Read and solve the problem.

In a Hula Hoop contest, four students twirl their Hula Hoops 89 times. Use the numbers below to write an addition sentence to show the number of times they twirl the Hula Hoops. You may use the numbers more than once.

0 2 4 6 8

1 3 5 7 9

1. What number sentence can you write?

☐☐ + ☐☐ + ☐☐ + ☐☐ = 89

2. Write a story problem about the number of times four students twirl their Hula Hoops.

____

____

____

____

____

Directions: Label *north, south, east*, and *west* on the compass rose. Then, use the compass rose to answer the questions.

1. Imagine you are walking north. If you make a right turn, in which direction are you now walking? ____________________

2. Imagine you are walking west. If you make a left turn, in which direction are you now walking? ____________________

3. Imagine you are walking south. If you make a right turn, in which direction are you now walking? ____________________

4. Imagine you are walking east. If you make a left turn, in which direction are you now walking? ____________________

Directions: Follow the steps in this experiment to discover which is bigger: hot air or cold air.

What You Need

- soda bottle
- balloon
- deep bowl
- cold water
- hot water
- ice

What to Do

1. Stretch out the balloon. Pull the neck of the balloon over the mouth of the bottle.
2. Fill the bowl halfway with hot water.
3. Hold the bottle with its bottom in the water for three minutes. Draw the bottle and the balloon below.
4. Pour the water into the sink. Stand the bottle in the bowl. Fill the bowl with ice.
5. Add cold water to the ice. Hold the bottle straight for three minutes. Draw the bottle and the balloon below.
6. The water changed the temperature of the air in the bottle.

Hot air takes up ________________ space than cold air.
(*more / less*)

Hot Water	Cold Water

Directions: Look at the word *teacher*. See how many words you can make using only the letters in *teacher*. Write the words below. Then, answer the questions.

Example: *tea*

__________ __________ __________

__________ __________ __________

__________ __________ __________

__________ __________ __________

1. How many words did you make?

____

2. Describe your strategy for making words.

____

____

Directions: Work with a partner. Use small objects to mark your spots on the game board. Take turns rolling a number cube. Move the number of spaces that you roll. If the space has words, follow those directions. The first person to reach the finish line wins.

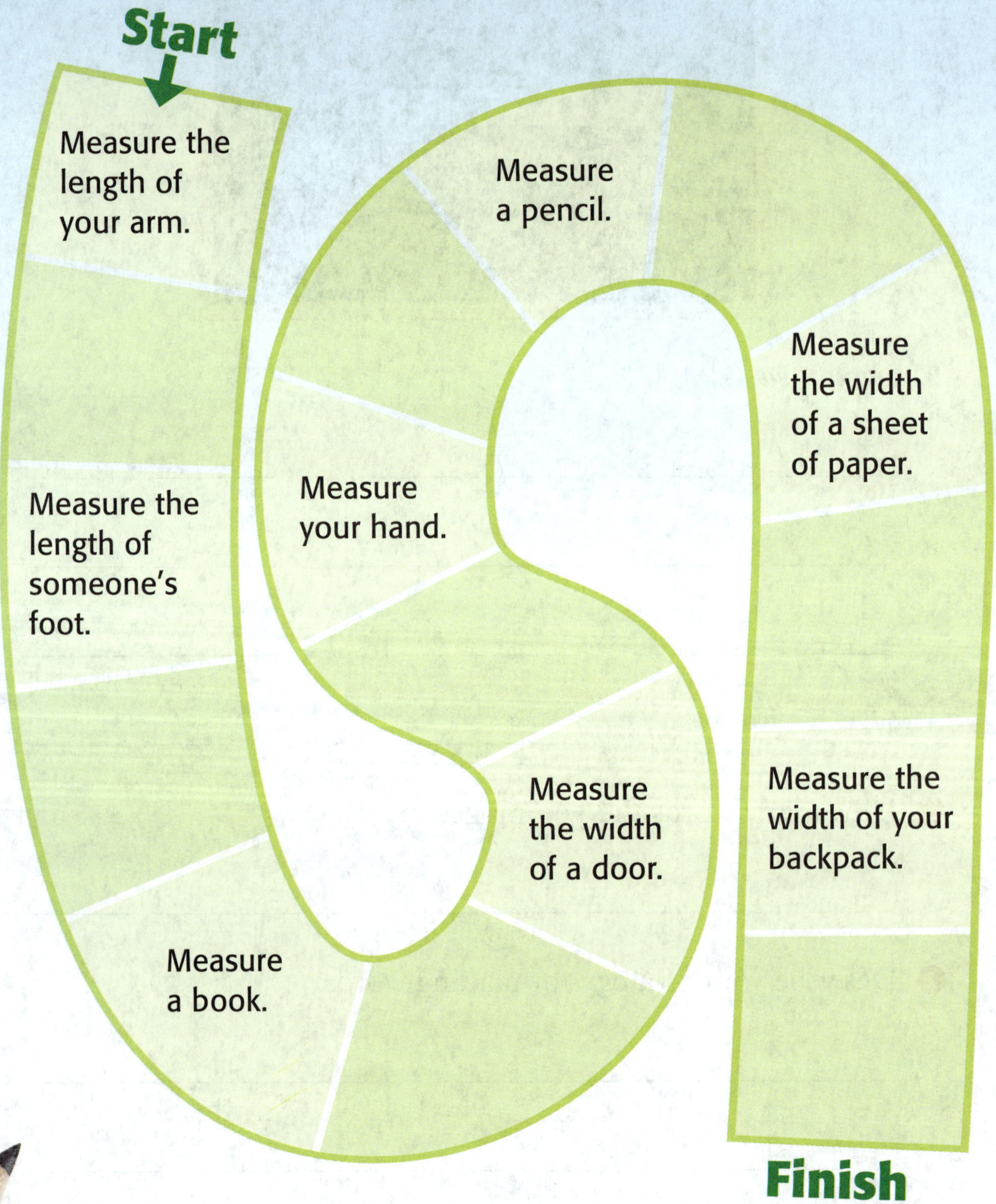

High-Frequency Words Activity

Use chalk to draw a hopscotch board on the sidewalk. Write one word from page 99 in each square. As you play, call out each word when you land in the square.

Mathematics Activity

Choose one problem from page 104. Use only drawings to show the problem and how you solved it.

Problem-Solving Activity

Create two addition problems like those on pages 105–106. Solve the problems using arrays.

Social Studies Activity

Choose a place in your community. Draw a map that shows how you get from your home to that place. Include a compass rose on your map. Hint: Look online or use a map application to find out where north is in your community.

Critical-Thinking Activity

Write your first and last name at the top of a sheet of paper. Then, write as many words as you can using only the letters from your name.

Listening-and-Speaking Activity

Use the map you created (see the social studies activity above) to tell a family member how to get to the place you chose. Include which way a person would turn and which direction they should go.

Directions: Read the text, and answer the questions on the next page.

American Indian Homes

American Indians live in tribes. These tribes live in different parts of the country. Long ago, they built homes that helped them survive. The homes were made with what the tribes had.

American Indians lived in many different types of homes. Tribes that lived on large, grassy plains used the grass to build homes. They worked well in warm climates. These structures were up to 40 feet (12 meters) tall!

Adobe homes were a different type of home. They were called *pueblos* (PWEB-lohz). These homes were made of clay and straw. They often had more than one story. They worked well for tribes who stayed in one place for a long time. Pueblos helped keep people cool in hot weather.

Plank houses worked well in cold climates. Tribes that lived in plank houses built them out of wood. The people found tall trees in nearby forests to make planks. Plank houses were also permanent houses.

Some tribes traveled a lot, so they built homes that could be easily moved. A tepee was one type of temporary home. A tepee looked like a tent. It was made of buffalo hide. Tribes that hunted buffalo built these homes.

All the tribes had to be smart builders. They used the materials they had nearby. They built homes to survive in many climates.

Directions: Read "American Indian Homes," and then answer the questions.

1. Which example shows the strongest connection to the text?
   - (A) I have grass in my backyard.
   - (B) Our house is built strong for hurricanes.
   - (C) I have never seen a plank house.
   - (D) I have seen buffalo at the zoo.

2. What type of house works well in a cold climate?
   - (A) a plank house
   - (B) a blank house
   - (C) a pink house
   - (D) a grass house

3. Based on context clues, what is a buffalo hide?
   - (A) the skin
   - (B) the teeth
   - (C) the feet
   - (D) the head

4. What do adobe and grass houses have in common?
   - (A) They are both easy to move.
   - (B) They are both made of grass.
   - (C) They both work well in warmer climates.
   - (D) They both use wood.

5. Which is the best summary of the text?
   - (A) Plank houses were made from wood.
   - (B) Tribes built homes that were easily moveable.
   - (C) Tribes built homes that met their needs.
   - (D) American Indians lived in tepees.

Directions: Write the correct word from the Word Bank to complete each sentence. Then, write your own sentence using one of the words.

Word Bank

• book	• once	• state	• late	• without
• hear	• carry	• miss	• second	• stop

1. My friend is moving to another ________________.
2. Do you ________________ that ringing noise?
3. I can play outside ________________ I finish my dinner.
4. Can you help me ________________ this heavy box?
5. The ________________ has sixteen chapters.
6. You must ________________ at the red light.
7. I was ________________ in line for lunch.
8. Dan likes french fries ________________ ketchup.
9. Susan woke up early so she would not be ________________.
10. I didn't want to ________________ the bus.

____

____

Directions: Answer each question.

1. Circle the words that need capital letters.

   the mississippi river flows for many miles.

2. Circle the words that need capital letters.

   i want to order a book from the scholastic®
   book order.

3. Write a sentence about a continent using correct capitalization.

   ____

   ____

4. Write a sentence about where you live using correct capitalization.

   ____

   ____

5. Which types of words are always capitalized? Circle the correct answer.

   names of countries   compound words   adjectives

6. Circle the words that need capital letters.

   can you canoe on lake michigan?

Directions: Write the names of two people to whom you have given gifts. Then, write words that tell how you felt when you gave the gifts.

To: ______________________________

I gave: ______________________________

How I felt when I gave this gift: ______________

____

____

To: ______________________________

I gave: ______________________________

How I felt when I gave this gift: ______________

____

____

Directions: Think about a time you gave someone a gift. Write a narrative about what the gift was, how you picked it out, and how the person reacted when they opened it. Use your notes on page 116 to help you.

Edit and Revise!

Be sure that you check your writing for:

- correct capitalization
- correct punctuation
- strong sensory details

Directions: Solve each problem.

1. $8 + 7 = \square + 9$
2. $9 + \square = 17 - 4$
3. $5 - 3 = \square - 6$
4. $10 + 3 = 7 + \square$
5. $\square - 5 = 7 - 3$
6. $\square - 3 = 7 + 5$
7. $9 - \square = 2 + 3$
8. $\square + 5 = 9 + 3$
9. $11 + 4 = 20 - \square$
10. $18 - \square = 12 + 2$
11. $17 + 2 = \square - 1$
12. $8 + 5 = 10 + \square$
13. $19 - 5 = \square + 7$
14. $13 - 2 = 20 - \square$

Directions: Solve each problem.

1. Write the missing number.

90	80		60	50

2. Eunice has 5 soccer games every month. How many games does she have after 4 months?

1 Month	2 Months	3 Months	4 Months
5	10	15	

3. Write the missing number.

15	20	25	30	

4. Tina's hair grows about 2 inches every month. About how many inches will her hair grow in 3 months?

1 Month	2 Months	3 Months
2		

5. Write the missing number.

30	40		60	70

6. Write the missing number.

11	13	15	17	

Unit 8

Problem Solving

Directions: Read and solve the problems.

0	1	2	3	4	5	6	7	8	9

1. Use the numbers in the squares to write an addition sentence that equals 981. Use the numbers only once.

   ☐☐☐ + ☐☐☐ = 981

2. Write a different number sentence from the same fact family.

   ☐☐☐ + ☐☐☐ = 981

3. Write two subtraction sentences from the same fact family.

   ☐☐☐ – ☐☐☐ = ☐☐☐

   ☐☐☐ – ☐☐☐ = ☐☐☐

Directions: Read and solve the problems.

1. Which tool can you use to measure the length of your pencil? Use the tool to measure.

   I measured a pencil with a ______________________.

   It is __________________ long.

2. Which tool can you use to measure the length of your finger? Use the tool to measure.

   I measured my finger with a ____________________.

   It is __________________ long.

3. Which tool can you use to measure the length of your shoe? Use the tool to measure.

   I measured my shoe with a ______________________.

   It is __________________ long.

4. Choose an object to measure to the nearest foot. Use a tool to measure.

   I measured a ________________________ with

   a __________________________.

   It is __________________ long.

Directions: On the chart, write two things that each person has the authority to do. Then, write one thing that each person does not have the authority to do.

Person	Authority To Do	Cannot Do
Example: doctor	give checkups put a cast on a broken arm	arrest people
teacher		
police officer		
crossing guard		
parent		
mayor		
president		

Directions: Follow the steps in this experiment to discover how things melt.

What You Need

- butter
- candle wax
- chocolate
- sugar
- foil
- scissors
- craft stick
- heat source

What to Do

1. Cut out four squares of foil. Fold the edges up to make flat trays.
2. Place butter in the first tray, candle wax in the second tray, chocolate in the third tray, and sugar in the fourth tray.
3. Have an adult heat each tray.
4. Watch the trays for five minutes. Draw what happens.

5. Have an adult turn off the heat source. Carefully stir each substance with the craft stick. Let them cool. Discuss what happened with the adult who helped you.

Directions: Read each step. Write the answer on the line next to each step. Use the previous number for the next step.

1. Start at the number 90. ______90______
2. Skip count by 2s five times. ____________
3. Subtract 31. ____________
4. Add 1. ____________
5. Skip count by 5s three times. ____________
6. Add 15. ____________
7. Subtract 10. ____________
8. What do you notice about your starting and ending numbers?

   ____
9. On a separate sheet of paper, make your own set of directions. What do you want the problem solver to notice after solving all of your problems?

Directions: Work with a partner. Take turns rolling a number cube two times per turn. The first roll tells you which column to look at. Then, roll again to tell you which row. Read the word in the column and row that you rolled. For example, if you roll a 6 and then a 2, you would read the word *night*. Cross out the square once you have read it. Keep playing until all the squares are crossed out.

	1	2	3	4	5	6
1	book	hear	once	carry	state	miss
2	late	second	without	stop	mile	night
3	walk	white	sea	began	river	four
4	grow	took	got	group	often	run
5	important	children	side	car	feet	until
6	country	every	add	plant	below	food

High-Frequency Words Activity

Write your own sentences for each word in the Word Bank on page 114. Then, rewrite your sentences leaving out the high-frequency words. Ask a family member to complete the sentences.

Mathematics Activity

Choose one series of numbers from page 119. Continue skip counting 10 more times from the last number in the series.

Problem-Solving Activity

Choose five items from your classroom or home. Measure the length of each object in inches. Then, measure the length of the object in centimeters.

Science Activity

Have an adult help you identify other materials that you can safely melt. Have an adult help you melt those materials. Write and draw what you observe. Observe what happens after they are removed from the heat. Do they become solid again? Can you make them solid again? If so, how?

Listening-and-Speaking Activity

Create a funny story about a community worker from page 122 who tries to do something he or she cannot do. Turn your story into a one-person skit to perform for your family.

Directions: Read the text, and answer the questions on the next page.

A New Hobby

The school band had sent home a notice to parents. They were looking for new students to join. The band teacher was excited for the band to grow. He promised to help students who had never played before.

José wanted to play an instrument. He had loved music his whole life. He loved singing and dancing. He also knew a little bit about reading music. Now, he was ready to join the band.

José was torn. He could not decide which instrument he wanted to learn how to play. His brother played the drums. His friend played the tuba. His neighbor played the clarinet. He thought those instruments were fun. But which one was the right one for him? José went to talk to the teacher, Mr. Riley. He was nervous. He hoped Mr. Riley would help him.

Mr. Riley told José that many students struggle to pick an instrument. It is a big decision. Band members spend a lot of time practicing and playing. They talked about the good and bad things about each choice. The tuba was heavy, but unique. The drums were not easy to move around, but they were fun to play. The clarinet was challenging, but had a great sound. In the end, José picked the saxophone! He joined the band. He loved learning about music.

Directions: Read "A New Hobby," and then answer the questions.

1. Who might make the strongest connection to the text?
   - (A) a kid who dislikes music
   - (B) a person who is choosing a second language to learn
   - (C) a person who likes music videos
   - (D) a kid named José

2. What is José going to join?
   - (A) the bond
   - (B) the bind
   - (C) the bend
   - (D) the band

3. What does the word *grow* mean in the first paragraph?
   - (A) get bigger
   - (B) get taller
   - (C) raise crops
   - (D) breed

4. What is the problem?
   - (A) José doesn't like music.
   - (B) José doesn't want to join the band.
   - (C) José doesn't know which instrument to play.
   - (D) José doesn't know where the band room is.

5. Which gives the best summary of the story?
   - (A) José likes the clarinet but settles for the tuba.
   - (B) José does not agree with the band teacher and does his own thing.
   - (C) José struggles to pick an instrument, but he chooses and has a great time.
   - (D) José's school band is in danger of being canceled, and then he decides to join.

Directions: Unscramble each word. Use the Word Bank to help you.

Word Bank

- idea
- face
- beautiful
- right
- because
- eat
- friend
- area
- watch
- enough

1. erdfin ______________________
2. reaa ______________________
3. irthg ______________________
4. eta ______________________
5. ngoeuh ______________________
6. daie ______________________
7. ctawh ______________________
8. cfea ______________________
9. cubseae ______________________
10. ufubetila ______________________

Directions: Read and answer each question.

1. Write the correct pronoun to complete the sentence.

   How did you hurt ____________________?
   (*myself*, *herself*, *yourself*)

2. Circle the pronoun in the sentence.

   The kids hid themselves in the forest.

3. Write the correct pronoun to complete the sentence.

   I can't hear ____________________ think when
   (*myself*, *herself*, *yourself*)
   it is this loud!

4. Write the correct pronoun to complete the sentence.

   I can make breakfast for ____________________.
   (*myself*, *herself*, *yourself*)

5. Write the correct pronoun to complete the sentence.

   "Students, clean up after ____________________,"
   (*ourselves*, *yourselves*, *yourself*)
   said the teacher.

6. Write the correct pronoun to complete the sentence.

   "What will I do with ____________________
   (*myself*, *herself*, *yourself*)
   today?" Ana wondered.

Directions: Read the facts about the two places. Form an opinion about which place you would like to visit. Write your opinion and your reasons below.

Facts

U.S.S. *Constitution*

- located in Boston, MA
- oldest U.S. naval ship still floating
- first sailed in 1797
- many other historical sites to see within walking distance of the U.S.S. *Constitution*

Mount Rushmore

- located in South Dakota
- faces of four U.S. presidents carved in stone
- there are many opportunities for hiking and exploring in the surrounding area
- the carving was completed in 1941

I would like to visit…

____

My Reasons:

____

____

____

____

____

Directions: Write a paragraph about a place that you would like to visit. Include reasons to support your opinions. Use the ideas on page 131 to help you.

Edit and Revise!

Be sure that you check your writing for:

- capital letters at the beginning of sentences
- capitalized proper nouns
- reasons and details that support your opinion

Directions: Solve each problem.

1. It is April 16, and Marco is already planning for his birthday that is exactly three months away. What date is Marco's birthday?

____

2. Mark reads 5 chapter books every month. How many books does he read in 3 months?

____

3. A group of cats has 16 legs. How many cats are there?

____

4. There are 9 mommy ducks. There are 43 ducklings. How many more ducklings are there than mommy ducks?

____

5. A van will hold 9 people. If a class of 23 students is going on a field trip, how many vans will be needed?

____

6. Kelly counts the cars that drive by her house. She counts 16 red cars, 13 blue cars, and 9 green cars. How many more red cars did Kelly see than green cars?

____

7. You have 53 trading cards. You lose 22 in a game. Then, you win 17. How many trading cards do you have now?

____

8. Deserea ran 15 miles last week. She ran 6 miles this week. How many miles did she run in all?

____

Directions: Solve each problem.

1. Write the numeral.

8	hundreds	4	tens	3	ones

____

2. Write the numeral.

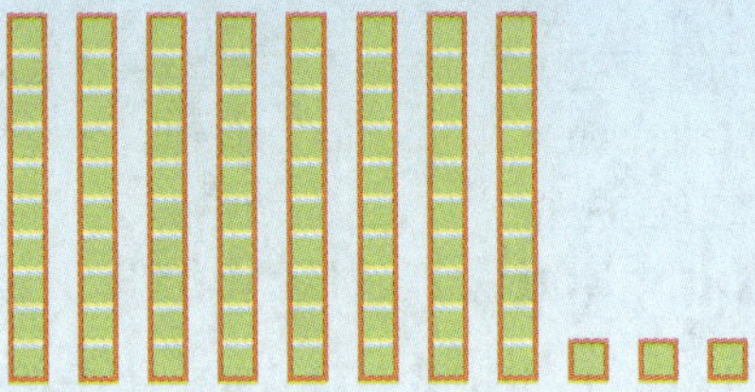

____

3. Write the numeral.

3	hundreds	0	tens	9	ones

____

4. Circle about how many children can fit on a school bus.

60 300

5. Write the ordinal number for six. ______________

6. Write the numeral.

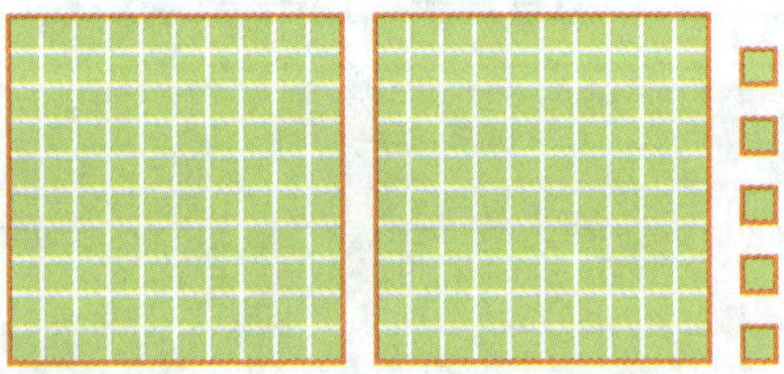

____

7. Circle groups of 2.

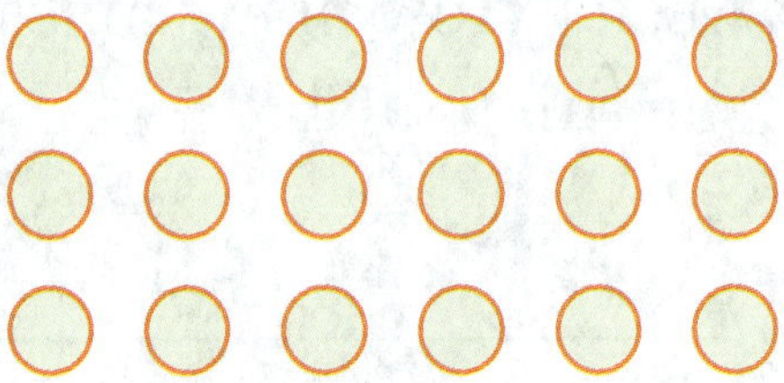

______________ groups

Directions: Read and solve the problem.

Francisco is using a number line to figure out how many minutes he watched a movie.

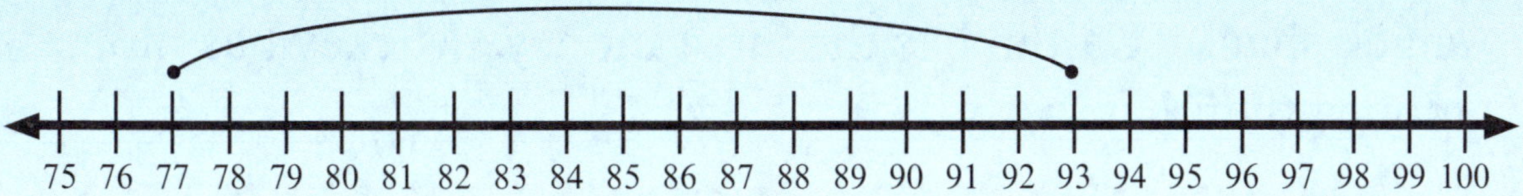

1. Write an addition sentence that can be solved using this number line. Explain your thinking.

2. Write a subtraction sentence that can be solved using this number line. Explain your thinking.

Directions: Read and solve the problem.

Caitlin, Mickey, and Kimberly have money to spend at a snack shack. Caitlin has the most money. Mickey has more money than Kimberly.

1. Complete the table to show the number of dollars and coins each person might have.

	Dollar	Quarter	Dime	Nickel	Penny	Total
Caitlin						
Mickey						
Kimberly						

2. Use the information from the table to write a story problem about the money each person has.

____

____

____

____

Directions: List characteristics for each type of place to live. Then, answer the questions.

Suburban (Suburbs)	Urban (City)	Rural (Country)

1. Which category best describes where you live? Why?

____

____

2. If you could live anywhere, which type of place would you choose to live? Why?

____

____

Directions: Follow the steps in this experiment to discover how a battery can make heat.

What You Need

- 3 cm x 15 cm (1 in. x 6 in.) strip of foil
- AA battery
- timer

What to Do

1. Fold the foil in half (hot dog style).
2. Fold the foil in half again (hot dog style). You have made a "wire."
3. Hold the battery with one hand. With the other hand, hold the ends of the "wire" against the ends of the battery for 10 seconds.
4. It feels ________________________ than before.
   (*the same, colder, hotter*)
5. Batteries store electric energy. The wire let this energy flow from the battery. Why did the wire's temperature change?

   ____

   ____

   ____

   ____

Directions: Read each set of words. Circle the word that does not belong. Then, explain your reasoning.

1. squirrel dog cat parrot

____

2. magazine computer newspaper book

____

3. sparrow eagle horse hummingbird

____

4. flute drums clarinet trumpet

____

5. pink red blue yellow

____

6. apple pear spinach peach

____

7. water coffee lemonade juice

____

8. sad happy excited glad

____

Directions: Remove the face cards and aces from a deck of cards. Then, shuffle the remaining cards. Place the stack facedown. Turn over three cards. Write a three-digit number that uses the numbers on the cards you drew. Then, write the expanded form and number form for each number.

Number	Expanded Form	Word Name
Example: 248	200 + 40 + 8	two hundred forty-eight

High-Frequency Words Activity

Write each word from the Word Bank on page 129 on a craft stick. Place the sticks in a cup or jar. Pull out one stick at a time, and read the word written on it. Continue until you have read all the words.

Mathematics Activity

Choose a three-digit number. How many ways can you show its value? Write, draw, and use objects to show it in as many ways as you can.

Social Studies Activity

Fold a sheet of drawing paper into three sections. Draw a picture to represent each of the following areas: rural, urban, suburban.

Critical-Thinking Activity

Sort the words from the Word Bank on page 129 into categories. Explain your reasoning for how the words fit into your categories. Then, sort the words a different way. How many different ways can you sort the words?

Listening-and-Speaking Activity

Ask your family members about places that are important to them. After they are finished, summarize their opinions in your own words.

Directions: Read the text, and answer the questions on the next page.

Natural Disasters

A natural disaster is often a sudden event. It is usually intense. It can have extreme results. It is caused by forces in nature. It might start with rain or heavy winds. A volcano erupts. The earth shakes. A tsunami hits the coast. These are all natural disasters.

Natural disasters can happen anywhere. They can occur at any time. Some areas are prone to big storms. Tsunamis are a worry for people who live by the ocean. It all depends on where you live.

Disasters can be scary. They often hurt or kill people. They can cause a lot of damage to homes and buildings. Entire towns can be ruined.

One way to handle a disaster is to plan ahead. Planning can keep us safe. It also gives us peace of mind to know we are ready. Other people help us prepare. Some places have warnings. They tell people to evacuate to a safe place. They let people know when a big disaster may be on the way. Other disasters happen too quickly. An earthquake can surprise you. There is no warning. An earthquake kit can help you after the event.

Where do you live? What happens in your town or city? Find out what you need. Make a plan with your family, and be ready!

Directions: Read "Natural Disasters," and then answer the questions.

1. Who might make the strongest connection to the text?
   - (A) a teacher who reads about tsunamis
   - (B) a mother who follows weather forecasts
   - (C) a boy who likes to watch waves in a storm
   - (D) a girl who has lived through a hurricane

2. Before a natural disaster occurs,
   - (A) plane ahead.
   - (B) plan ahead.
   - (C) pan ahead.
   - (D) plot ahead.

3. What does the word *prone* mean?
   - (A) will occur
   - (B) likely to occur
   - (C) won't occur
   - (D) cannot occur

4. Which is the main idea of this text?
   - (A) disaster predicting
   - (B) disaster reporting
   - (C) disaster preparedness
   - (D) disaster warnings

5. Which gives the best summary of the text?
   - (A) Hurricanes occur only in certain places.
   - (B) Preparing for a tornado takes a lot of time.
   - (C) Preparing for a natural disaster is a smart thing to do.
   - (D) People far from the coast don't need to worry about tsunamis.

Directions: Write a sentence that uses the word in each box.

1. young ______________________________

2. talk ______________________________

3. soon ______________________________

4. list ______________________________

5. song ______________________________

6. small ______________________________

7. large ______________________________

8. outside ______________________________

9. sometimes ______________________________

10. another ______________________________

Directions: Answer each question.

1. Rewrite the sentence in the past tense.

   I wake up in the morning when the sun comes up.

   ____

   ____

2. Write the past tense word to complete the sentence.

   The boss ____________ *(pay)* his workers once a month.

3. Circle the past tense of *catch*.

   catched   catchy   caught

4. Write the correct verb to complete the sentence.

   The baby piglet ____________ *(find, found)* his mother and cuddled with her.

5. Write the past tense word to complete the sentence.

   Yesterday, I ____________ *(mean)* to get my bag, but I forgot it.

6. Circle the past tense of *write*.

   wrate   wrote   writing

Directions: Place check marks in the icebergs with facts about penguins. Add any more facts that you know about penguins.

Penguins live where it is very cold.

Penguins are cute.

You can find penguins in the water but not in the sky.

It is fun to watch penguins move.

Each set of penguins has one or two babies a year.

Penguins can swim, but they cannot fly.

____

____

____

____

____

____

Directions: Write a paragraph about penguins. Include facts about where they live and their physical characteristics. Use your notes from page 146 to help you.

Edit and Revise!

Be sure that you check your writing for:

- capital letters at the beginning of sentences
- capitalized proper nouns
- details that support your main idea

Directions: Solve each problem.

1. Is a car longer or shorter than a yard?

____

2. Circle the better estimate for the width.

2 m   10 m

3. Is a ladder less than 1 meter, about 1 meter, or more than 1 meter?

____

4. Is a cat longer or shorter than a yard?

____

5. Circle the object that is shorter than 1 meter.

6. Circle the object that would be taller than 1 meter.

7. Is a goldfish longer or shorter than 1 foot?

____

8. Is a chair less than 1 meter, about 1 meter, or more than 1 meter tall?

____

Directions: Solve each problem.

1. 84 + 14 = ________

2. 118 – 29 = ________

3.
$$\begin{array}{r} 71 \\ +\ \ 52 \\ \hline \end{array}$$
□

4. 142 – 139 = ________

5.
$$\begin{array}{r} 172 \\ +\ 163 \\ \hline \end{array}$$
□

6. 32 plus 22 equals ________________.

7. 67 minus 50 equals ________________.

8.
$$\begin{array}{r} 208 \\ -\ \ 61 \\ \hline \end{array}$$
□

9. 644 + 92 = ________

10.
$$\begin{array}{r} 434 \\ -\ 280 \\ \hline \end{array}$$
□

Directions: Read and solve the problem.

Laura and her friends were playing football. Use the information below to find the number of yards each girl threw the football.

- Laura threw the football 3 yards.
- Maria threw the football 2 more yards than Laura.
- Sarah threw the football 3 fewer yards than Maria.
- Jean threw the football the same number of yards Laura and Sarah threw the football combined.

1. Show the number of yards each girl threw the football in the table.
2. Make a bar graph to show the data.

Girl	Yards
Laura	
Maria	
Sarah	
Jean	

Title: ______________________________

________ ________ ________ ________

____

Directions: Read and solve the problem.

Marissa has a paper triangle. She wants to partition it into smaller triangles. How can Marissa partition her triangle into equal parts?

1. Show three ways to partition the triangle into halves. How many halves does each triangle have?

_______________ halves

2. Show how to partition the triangle into thirds. How many thirds are there?

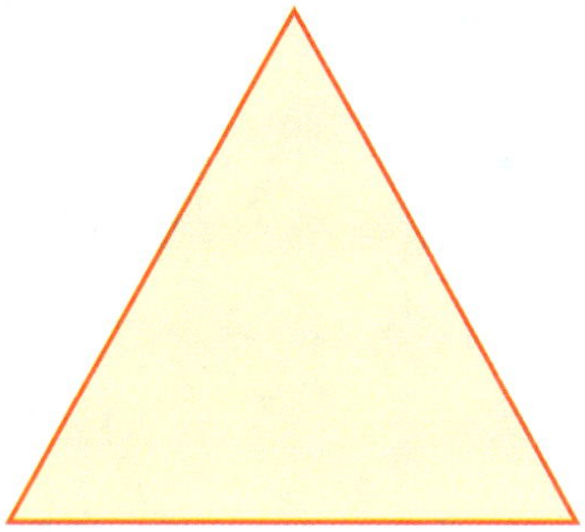

_______________ thirds

3. Show how to partition the triangle into fourths. How many fourths are there?

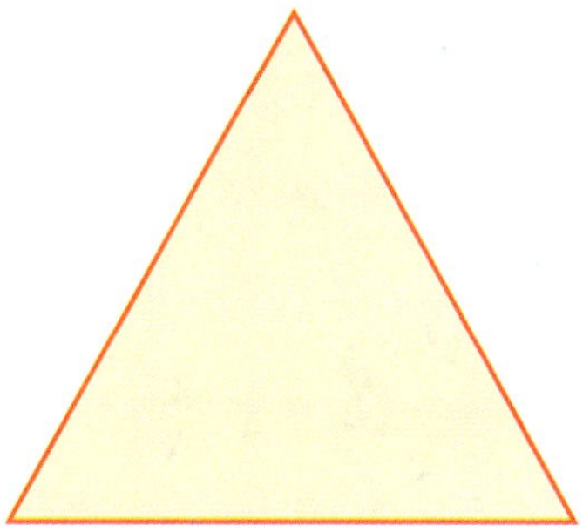

_______________ fourths

Directions: Pretend that you are running for president of the United States. Create a campaign poster that tells why you will be a good president. Include information about at least one way that you will put the needs and interests of others ahead of your own.

________________________ **for President**

(Your Name)

Directions: Follow the steps in this experiment to discover which things are magnetic.

What You Need

- magnet
- paper clips
- marbles
- nuts and bolts
- nails
- aluminum foil
- pebbles
- string
- blocks
- other metal and non-metal items
- scraps of paper

What to Do

1. Using a magnet, test each object to see whether it is magnetic.
2. Make a chart to record your results as you test each item.
3. What did all of the magnetic items have in common?

   ____

4. What happened when the magnet got near these items?

   ____

   ____

5. Describe the items that were attracted to the magnet. Why do you think they were attracted while others were not?

   ____

   ____

Directions: Look at each shape. Decide how many different ways you can divide each shape into equal parts. Use a different color pen to show each way you can divide the shape.

1

2

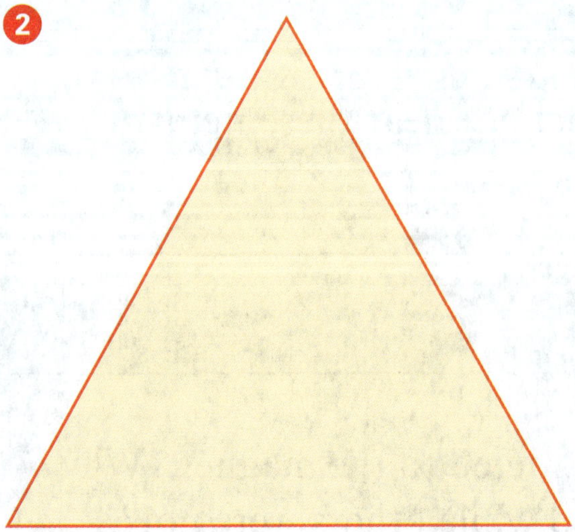

3

4

Directions: Remove the face cards and aces from a deck of cards. Then, shuffle the remaining cards. Take turns with a partner turning over two cards from the top of the deck. Write the value of each card on the left. Write the sum of the two cards on the right. The person with the highest sum wins.

Cards	Sum
_____ + _____	
_____ + _____	
_____ + _____	
_____ + _____	
_____ + _____	
_____ + _____	
_____ + _____	
_____ + _____	
_____ + _____	
_____ + _____	
_____ + _____	
_____ + _____	

High-Frequency Words Activity

Write each word from page 144 on an index card. Tape each index card to a wall. Turn out the lights. Have someone shine a flashlight on the cards, one at a time. Read each word that the light shines on.

Mathematics Activity

Measure a desk in feet. Then, measure it in meters. What do you notice about the two measurements? Explain your thinking to a family member.

Social Studies Activity

Write a speech stating why you would be a good president. Use the speech and the campaign poster from page 152 to convince your family that you would be a good president.

Critical-Thinking Activity

Draw a star with five points. Decide how many ways you can divide the star into equal parts. Explain your thinking to a family member.

Listening-and-Speaking Activity

Ask your family members what they know about penguins. Add this information to your paragraph from the writing activity. Then, read your finished paragraph aloud.

Answer Key

There are many open-ended pages, problems, and writing prompts in this book. For those activities, the answers will vary. Answers are only given in this answer key if they are specific.

page 7

1. D
2. C
3. A
4. C

page 8

1. B
2. D
3. D
4. C

page 9

1.	country	yrtnuoc
2.	every	yreve
3.	add	dda
4.	plant	tnalp
5.	below	woleb
6.	food	doof
7.	between	neewteb
8.	last	tsal
9.	near	raen
10.	own	nwo

page 10

1. flight
2. taught
3. square
4. brought
5. fixture
6. clown
7. needed
8. each
9. watch
10. fence

page 13

1. 3
2. 9
3. 10
4. 2
5. 0
6. 8
7. 5
8. 9
9. 6
10. 2

page 14

1. 50
2. 235
3. 39
4. 38
5. 67
6. 42
7. 93
8. seventy-one

page 15

Number	Hundreds	Tens	Ones
165			
253			

page 16

1.

Strategy 1: 23 tens blocks and 6 ones blocks

Strategy 2: 2 hundreds blocks, 3 tens blocks, and 6 ones blocks

2. Possible answer: In Strategy 1, there are 23 tens and 6 ones. In Strategy 2, there are 2 hundreds, 3 tens, and 6 ones. In Strategy 2, 10 tens are grouped to make 1 hundred.

page 17

People: car, bus, bicycle, scooter
Goods: cargo ship, delivery truck
Both: train, airplane

page 18

The first drawing should indicate that the ice floats and that most of the ice is below the water. The second drawing should indicate that the water is still at the line even though the ice has melted.

page 19

1. 326
2. square
3. 5
4. 24
5. hexagon
6. 23

page 22

1. B
2. B
3. D
4. A

page 23

1. A
2. C
3. A
4. D

page 24

1. keep; house; A
2. school; people; A
3. climbed; tree; B
4. father; brother; A
5. never; morning; A

page 25

1. A
2. B
3. A
4. C
5. A
6. C
7. C
8. C

page 28

1. tens
2. 643
3. 46
4. 148
5. 417
6. 356
7. 272
8. 582

page 29

1. 5 sides
2. 
3. 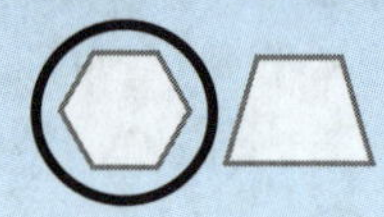
4. false
5. 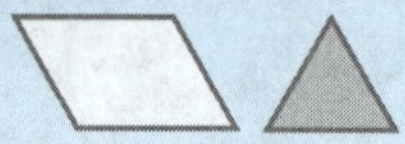
6. 
7. true

page 30

1. 2 hundreds, 6 tens, 8 ones. The number is 268.
2. 4 hundreds, 2 tens, 3 ones. The number is 423.

page 31

1. Strategy 1: 800 + 40 + 2; Strategy 2: 842
2. Possible answer: In Strategy 1, the values of each digit are being added together to show the number. In Strategy 2, the values of each digit are shown using place value.

page 34

page 37

1. D
2. C
3. B
4. B

page 38

1. C
2. D
3. B
4. A

page 39

1. light
2. eye
3. city
4. start

page 40

1. A
2. B
3. C
4. A
5. A
6. C
7. B
8. A

page 43

1.  
2.  
3. taller
4. 2 meters
5.  
6. more than 1 meter
7. 1 meter

page 44

1. half past 8:00
2. 6:30
3. half past 10:00
4. 
5. 
6. 2:00
7. 8:30
8. 

page 45

1. One cow weighs 732 pounds, and another cow weighs 832 pounds.
2. I need to find the cow that weighs more.
3. 732 = 7 hundreds, 3 tens, and 2 ones
   832 = 8 hundreds, 3 tens, and 2 ones
4. <

page 46

One cow weighs 951 pounds, and another cow weighs 915 pounds; Plans should explain how to use base-ten concepts to compare the two numbers; 951 (>) 915; Explanations should include how the value in the tens place is higher in 951 than in 915.

page 48

Responses should indicate that the moon changes shapes over the course of the month.

page 50

My mom is very sick.

When will you be back at school?

How many baseball cards do you have?

Marta walked to the store.

I can't wait to go camping!

Did you finish your homework?

Where is he going?

My favorite ice cream flavor is chocolate.

That's exciting!

Will you help me carry this heavy box?

Ouch!

How can I help you?

I do not feel well.

Science is my favorite subject.

Are we there yet?

page 52

1. C
2. B
3. C
4. D

page 53

1. B
2. C
3. B
4. C

page 54

1. fast
2. few
3. how
4. along
5. slow
6. with
7. left
8. while
9. next
10. them

page 55

1. Mario's pool felt very refreshing on a hot day.
2. Drivers don't always know when a car's gas is almost out.
3. doesn't, won't, haven't
4. should've
5. the flower's petal

page 58

1. Brenda
2. Ginny
3. 15 trains
4. Tracy and Mike

page 59

1. $6 - 1 = 5$
2. $7 - 3 = 4$
3. $7 - 4 = 3$
4. $6 - 5 = 1$
5. $5 - 1 = 4$
6. $8 - 5 = 3$
7. $7 - 2 = 5$
8. $6 - 4 = 2$

page 60

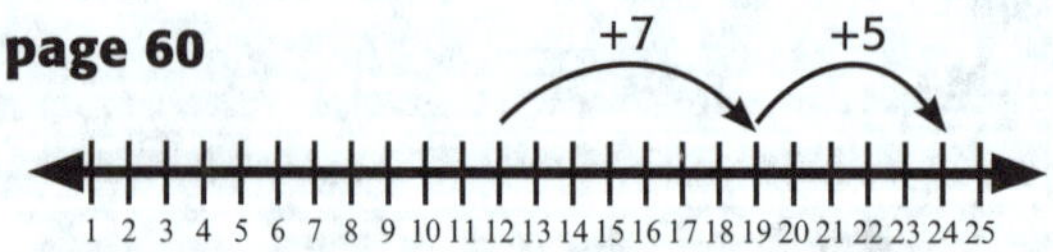

1. $12 + 7 = 19$
2. $19 + 5 = 24$

page 61

1. 38 crayons; Strategy 1: 26 circles should be colored red and 12 circles should be colored blue to show a total of 38; Strategy 2: student should have counted on 12 more from 26: 26, 27, 28, 29, 30, 31, 32, 33, 34, 35, 36, 37, 38
2. Possible answer: I think counting on is easier because if I start on 26, then I just count on 12 more. Counting on is faster than coloring in the ten frames and then counting them all up.

page 62

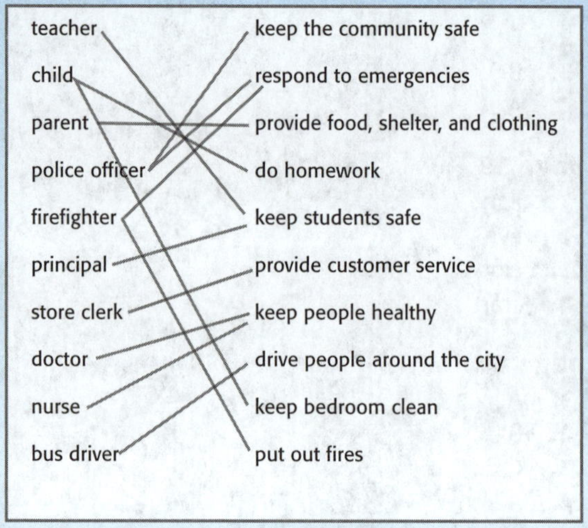

page 64

1. big bad wolf
2. get in shape
3. broken promise
4. stand by me
5. slow down
6. misunderstood

page 67

1. B
2. A
3. D
4. B

page 68

1. B
2. D
3. B
4. D

page 69

1. hard
2. begin
3. life
4. open
5. example
6. paper
7. Always
8. both
9. those
10. together

page 70

1. Example: A swarm of bees moved quickly.
2. Example: The young children rode the bus to school.
3. lovingly, quickly
4. Example: A bunch of leaves fell onto the driveway.
5. Example: A litter of puppies ran clumsily.
6. Example: A choir of students sang beautifully.

page 71

Turtles are reptiles.
Turtles lay eggs.
Some turtles live on land and others in water.
Turtles have upper and lower shells.
Turtle shells have different designs.
Turtles are cold blooded.

page 73

1. 46
2. 21
3. 39
4. 65
5. 26
6. 18

page 74

1. 75¢
2. 37
3. 9
4. 7
5. 38¢
6. $1.75
7. No
8. 62¢

page 75

1. Olivia scores 89 points in the first video game she plays and 57 points in the second video game.
2. I need to find the difference between the points Olivia scores in the two video games.
3. Possible answer: I will write a subtraction sentence to find the difference between the points Olivia scores in the video games.
4. 32 points

page 76

Jason scores 94 points on the first video game he plays and scores 72 points on the second video game; write a subtraction sentence to find the difference between the points he scores on the video games; 94 – 72 = 22; explanations should describe how students found the difference between the two scores.

page 78

Observations should include that water has gathered in the small container.

page 79

1. monkey
2. muffin
3. mosquito
4. melt
5. mad
6. magnify
7. messy
8. meadow

page 83

1. D
2. B
3. C
4. A
5. B

page 84

1. got tog
2. group puorg
3. often netfo
4. run nur
5. important tnatropmi
6. children nerdlihc
7. side edis
8. car rac
9. feet teef
10. until litnu

page 85

1. Dear Coach, Your player,
2. Example:
   Sincerely,
   Robert
3. Dear Dad, Your son,
4. Dear Luis, Your friend,

page 88

1. 86
2. 11
3. 118
4. 22
5. 99
6. 15
7. 16
8. 93
9. 96
10. 63
11. 74
12. 7

page 89

1. 4 angles
2. false
3. 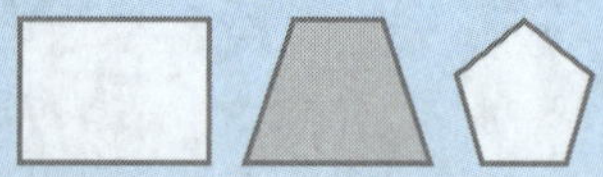
4. oval
5. 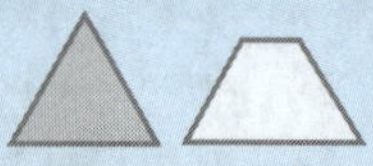
6. 5 angles
7. cube, rectangular prism, or square prism
8. circle

page 90

1. 54 – 12 = 42 miles per hour
2. 54 + 42 = 96 miles per hour
3. Possible strategies: number line; base-ten blocks; addition problem using place value

page 91

1. Possible answer: 30 + 27 + 31 = 88
2. Possible strategies: number line, base-ten blocks, equations, ten frames

page 94

There are 13 triangles.

page 98

1. B
2. C
3. D
4. C
5. B

page 100

1. Example: tall
2. the, happy, young
3. the, lifelong, the, intense
4. Example: enormous
5. Example: new
6. the, surprise, a, fun

page 103

1. 3 inches
2. ruler
3. 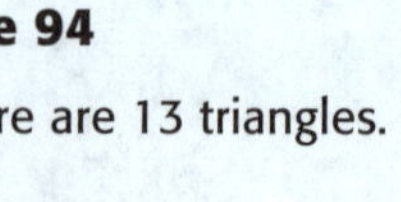
4. 
5. 3 centimeters
6. 2 inches
7. 
8. 5 centimeters

page 104

1. $<$
2. 405, 450, 504
3. 321, 234, 231
4. $>$
5. 756, 675, 75
6. =
7. 820, 823, 832
8. $<$

page 105

Possible arrays and addition sentences: 2 rows of 12, 12 + 12 = 24; 12 rows of 2, 2 + 2 + 2 + 2 + 2 + 2 + 2 + 2 + 2 + 2 + 2 + 2 = 24; 3 rows of 8, 8 + 8 + 8 = 24; 8 rows of 3, 3 + 3 + 3 + 3 + 3 + 3 + 3 + 3 = 24; 4 rows of 6, 6 + 6 + 6 + 6 = 24; 6 rows of 4, 4 + 4 + 4 + 4 + 4 + 4 = 24; 1 row of 24; 24 + 0 = 24; 24 rows of 1, 1 + 1 + 1 + 1 + 1 + 1 + 1 + 1 + 1 + 1 + 1 + 1 + 1 + 1 + 1 + 1 + 1 + 1 + 1 + 1 + 1 + 1 + 1 + 1 = 24

page 106

1. Possible answer: 20 + 21 + 22 + 26 = 89
2. Possible story problem: William, Henry, Mindy, and Tonya twirl a Hula Hoop. William twirls the Hula Hoop 20 times. Henry twirls the Hula Hoop 21 times. Mindy twirls the Hula Hoop 22 times. Tonya twirls the Hula Hoop 26 times. How many times did all four students twirl the Hula Hoop?

page 107

1. east
2. south
3. west
4. north

page 108

Drawings should reflect that the balloon inflated while the bottle was in hot water and deflated while the bottle was in cold water.

page 109

Possible answers include: *tea, teach, cheer, ache, reach, chart, tar, art, cheat, eat, rat, hat, cat, chat, char, act, tear, heat*

page 113

1. B
2. A
3. A
4. C
5. C

page 114

1. state
2. hear
3. once
4. carry
5. book
6. stop
7. second
8. without
9. late
10. miss

page 115

1. The, Mississippi, River
2. I, Scholastic
3. Example: My uncle told me about his trip to South America.
4. Example: I live in Atlanta, Georgia.
5. names of countries
6. Can, Lake Michigan

page 118

1. 6
2. 4
3. 8
4. 6
5. 9
6. 15
7. 4
8. 7
9. 5
10. 4
11. 20
12. 3
13. 7
14. 9

page 119

1. 70
2. 20 games
3. 35
4. 6 inches
5. 50
6. 19

page 120

1. Possible answer: 420 + 561 = 981
2. Possible answer: 561 + 420 = 981
3. Possible answer: 981 – 561 = 420 and 981 – 420 = 561

page 124

1. 90
2. 100
3. 69
4. 70
5. 85
6. 100
7. 90
8. They are the same number.

page 128

1. B
2. D
3. A
4. C
5. C

page 129

1. friend
2. area
3. right
4. eat
5. enough
6. idea
7. watch
8. face
9. because
10. beautiful

page 130

1. yourself
2. themselves
3. myself
4. myself
5. yourselves
6. myself

page 133

1. July 16th
2. 15
3. 4
4. 34
5. 3
6. 7
7. 48
8. 21

page 134

1. 843
2. 83
3. 309
4. 60
5. 6th or sixth
6. 205
7. 9

page 135

1. Possible answers: 77 + 16 = 93;
   77 + 10 + 6 = 93; 77 + 3 + 10 + 3 = 93
2. Possible answers: 93 − 16 = 77;
   93 − 3 − 13 = 77; 93 − 3 − 10 − 3 = 77

page 136

1. Accept any answer that shows Caitlin has the most money and Mickey has more money than Kimberly.
2. Possible story problem: Caitlin has $1.97 to spend at the snack shack. Mickey has $1.17 to spend at the snack shack. Kimberly has $0.53 to spend at the snack shack. How much more money does Caitlin have than Mickey? How much more money does Mickey have than Kimberly?

page 143

1. D
2. B
3. B
4. C
5. C

page 145

1. I woke up in the morning when the sun came up.
2. paid
3. caught
4. found
5. meant
6. wrote

page 146

Penguins live where it is very cold.
You can find penguins in the water but not in the sky.
Each set of penguins has one or two babies a year.
Penguins can swim, but they cannot fly.

page 148

1. longer
2. 2 m
3. more than 1 meter
4. shorter
5. 
6. 
7. shorter
8. about 1 meter

page 149

1. 98
2. 89
3. 123
4. 3
5. 335
6. 54
7. 17
8. 147
9. 736
10. 154

page 150

Girl	Yards
Laura	3
Maria	5
Sarah	2
Jean	5

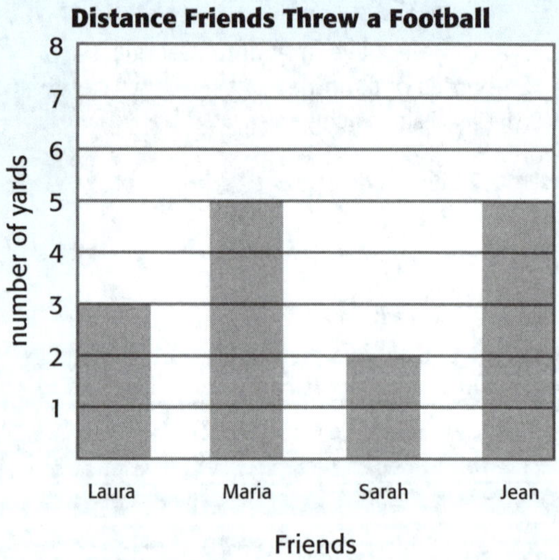

page 151

1. two halves
   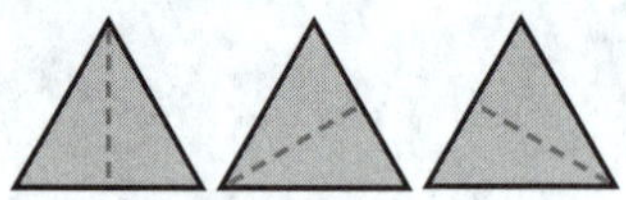
2. three thirds
   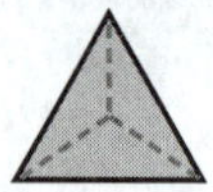
3. four fourths
   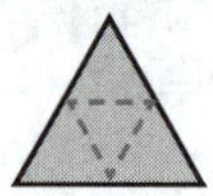

Skills and Standards in This Book

Today's standards have created more consistency in how mathematics and English language arts are taught. In the past, states and school districts had their own standards for each grade level. However, what was taught at a specific grade in one location may have been taught at a different grade in another location. This made it difficult when students moved.

Today, many states and school districts have adopted new standards. This means that for the first time, there is greater consistency in what is being taught at each grade level, with the ultimate goal of getting students ready to be successful in college and in their careers.

Standards Features

The overall goal for the standards is to better prepare students for life. Today's standards have several key features:

- They describe what students should know and be able to do at each grade level.
- They are rigorous and dive deeply into the content.
- They require higher-level thinking and analysis.
- They require students to explain and justify answers.
- They are aimed at making sure students are prepared for college and/or their future careers.

Unit Outline

This book is designed to help your child meet today's rigorous standards. This section describes the standards-based skills covered in each unit of study.

Unit 1	• Read and answer questions about a narrative and a piece of nonfiction text. • Practice reading and writing high-frequency words. • Identify common spelling patterns. • Write a narrative about playing with a friend.	• Add and subtract within 20. • Understand place value. • Identify modes of transportation. • Understand that water can change phases, while its volume stays the same.
Unit 2	• Read and answer questions about a narrative and a piece of nonfiction text. • Practice reading and writing high-frequency words. • Use an apostrophe to form contractions. • Write an opinion paragraph about scarecrows.	• Understand place value. • Identify shapes, their sides, and their vertices. • Understand the characteristics of a good leader. • Observe the composition of rocks.
Unit 3	• Read and answer questions about a narrative and a piece of nonfiction text. • Practice reading and writing high-frequency words. • Use frequently occurring irregular plural nouns. • Write a narrative about a bad day.	• Use place value to compare numbers. • Estimate lengths of objects. • Use digital and analog clocks to tell time. • Draw a map of the neighborhood. • Observe the phases of the moon.
Unit 4	• Read and answer questions about a narrative and a piece of nonfiction text. • Practice reading and writing high-frequency words. • Use an apostrophe to form contractions. • Write an opinion paragraph about the beach or the park. • Solve addition and subtraction word problems.	• Use tables and bar graphs to solve problems. • Use concrete models to add and subtract. • Understand what various people are responsible for. • Record observable properties.
Unit 5	• Read and answer questions about a narrative and a piece of nonfiction text. • Practice reading and writing high-frequency words. • Use adjectives and adverbs correctly. • Write an informative paragraph about turtles.	• Solve addition and subtraction word problems. • Solve word problems involving money. • Identify the local area on a map. • Observe that water is stored in leaves.

Unit 6	• Read and answer questions about a piece of nonfiction text. • Practice reading and writing high-frequency words. • Use commas in letters. • Write an opinion paragraph about eating apples.	• Fluently add and subtract within 100. • Solve addition and subtraction word problems. • Recognize two- and three-dimensional shapes. • Understand the meaning of justice. • Observe the local environment.
Unit 7	• Read and answer questions about a narrative. • Practice reading and writing high-frequency words. • Identify and use adjectives. • Write an informative paragraph about pushing and pulling. • Measure and compare lengths of objects.	• Use place value to compare numbers. • Solve addition and subtraction word problems. • Understand cardinal directions. • Understand that warm air has more volume than cold air.
Unit 8	• Read and answer questions about a piece of nonfiction text. • Practice reading and writing high-frequency words. • Use correct capitalization. • Write a narrative about giving a gift. • Skip count by 2s, 5s, and 10s. • Fluently add and subtract within 100.	• Use concrete models to add and subtract within 1,000. • Use appropriate tools to measure objects. • Understand who has authority and the limits of that authority. • Observe how things melt and that some things cannot become solid again.
Unit 9	• Read and answer questions about a narrative. • Practice reading and writing high-frequency words. • Use reflexive pronouns. • Write an opinion paragraph about a place to visit. • Solve addition and subtraction word problems.	• Understand place value within 1,000. • Use number lines to represent addition and subtraction. • Solve word problems involving money. • Understand the differences between urban, suburban, and rural areas. • Understand that electricity produces heat.
Unit 10	• Read and answer questions about a piece of nonfiction text. • Practice reading and writing high-frequency words. • Use frequently occurring irregular past tense verbs. • Write an informative paragraph about penguins.	• Add and subtract within 1,000. • Partition shapes into halves, thirds, and quarters. • Create a table and a bar graph to solve a problem. • Understand that a leader puts the interests of others first. • Observe properties of magnetic items.

Congratulations

______________________________________!

(name)

You have completed

Conquering Second Grade!

presented on ____________________

(date)